Digital Imaging

Edited by Muhammad Sarfraz

Published in London, United Kingdom

IntechOpen

Supporting open minds since 2005

Digital Imaging
http://dx.doi.org/10.5772/intechopen.83239
Edited by Muhammad Sarfraz

Contributors
Randa Khemiri, Nejmeddine Bahri, Mohamed Atri, Fatma Belghith, Soulef Bouaafia, Fatma Elzahra Sayadi, Nouri Masmoudi, Alonso Saldaña Heredia, Pedro Antonio Marquez Aguilar, Álvaro Zamudio Lara, Arturo Molina Ocampo, Touhami Tahenni, Edgar Mario Rico Mesa, Jhon Edison Goez Mora, Juan Camilo Londoño Lopera, Yomin Estiven Jaramillo Múnera, Riki Greenberg, Muhammad Sarfraz

First published in London, United Kingdom, 2020 by IntechOpen
IntechOpen is the global imprint of INTECHOPEN LIMITED, registered in England and Wales, registration number: 11086078, 7th floor, 10 Lower Thames Street, London, EC3R 6AF, United Kingdom
Printed in Croatia

British Library Cataloguing-in-Publication Data
A catalogue record for this book is available from the British Library

Additional hard and PDF copies can be obtained from orders@intechopen.com

Digital Imaging
Edited by Muhammad Sarfraz
p. cm.
Print ISBN 978-1-78985-599-9
Online ISBN 978-1-78985-600-2
eBook (PDF) ISBN 978-1-83880-389-6

For EU product safety concerns:
IN TECH d.o.o., Prolaz Marije Krucifikse Kozulić 3, 51000 Rijeka, Croatia, info@intechopen.com or visit our website at intechopen.com.

Meet the editor

Muhammad Sarfraz is Professor and Director of MSIT in the Department of Information Science, Kuwait University, Kuwait. His research interests include computer graphics, computer vision, image processing, machine learning, pattern recognition, soft computing, data science, intelligent systems, information technology, and information systems. Prof. Sarfraz has been a keynote/invited speaker at various platforms around the globe. He has advised more than 85 students for their MSc and PhD theses. He has published more than 350 publications as books, journals, and conference papers. Prof. Sarfraz is a member of various professional societies. He is the chair and member of the international advisory committees and organizing committees of various international conferences. He is also editor-in-chief and editor of various international journals.

Contents

Preface **XI**

Chapter 1 **1**
Introductory Chapter: On Digital Image Processing
by Muhammad Sarfraz

Chapter 2 **11**
Fast Motion Estimation's Configuration Using Diamond Pattern and ECU, CFM, and ESD Modes for Reducing HEVC Computational Complexity
by Randa Khemiri, Nejmeddine Bahri, Fatma Belghith, Soulef Bouaafia, Fatma Elzahra Sayadi, Mohamed Atri and Nouri Masmoudi

Chapter 3 **29**
Digital Image Processing Applied to Optical Measurements
by Alonso Saldaña-Heredia, Pedro Antonio Márquez-Aguilar, Álvaro Zamudio Lara and Arturo Molina-Ocampo

Chapter 4 **45**
Experimental and Theoretical Investigation on the Shear Behaviour of High Strength Reinforced Concrete Beams Using Digital Image Correlation
by Touhami Tahenni and Thibaut Lecompte

Chapter 5 **63**
Implementation of an Artificial Vision System for Welding in the Retrofitting Process of a Robotic Arm Industrial
by Yomin Estiven Jaramillo Munera, Jhon Edison Goez Mora, Juan Camilo Londoño Lopera and Edgar Mario Rico Mesa

Chapter 6 **75**
EBSCO Discovery Service (EDS) Usage in Israeli Academic Libraries
by Riki Greenberg

Preface

Currently, digital imaging is used widely in various real-life applications. There are a number of potential digital imaging applications such as television, photography, robotics, remote sensing, medical diagnosis, reconnaissance, architectural and engineering design, art, crime prevention, geographical information systems, communication, intellectual property, retail catalogs, nudity detection, face finding, industrial, and others. The increasing trends, needs, and applications of imaging make it more difficult to process images for desired objectives. This leads to the idea of capturing, storing, finding, retrieving, analyzing, and using images in everyday life in the computing environment. Being a computer-based technology, digital imaging carries out automatic processing, manipulation, and interpretation of visual information. It plays a significant and important role in various aspects of real life. It is also highly useful in many areas, disciplines, and fields of art, science, and technology.

This book is specifically dedicated to digital imaging education, research, applications, techniques, tools, and algorithms that originate from fields such as image processing, computer vision, pattern recognition, signal processing, artificial intelligence, intelligent systems, and soft computing. In general, this comprehensive book contains state-of-the-art chapters focusing on the latest developments using theories, methods, approaches, algorithms, analyses, display of images, visual information, and videos.

The six chapters from academicians, practitioners, and researchers from different disciplines of life explore the latest developments, methods, approaches, and applications of digital imaging in a variety of fields and endeavors. The book is compiled with a view to providing researchers, academicians, and readers with an in-depth discussion of the latest advances.

The target audience of this book are professionals and researchers working in the field of digital imaging in various disciplines, e.g. computer science, computer engineering, information technology, information and communication sciences, education, health, libraries, and others. The book is also targeted at scientists, engineers, researchers, practitioners, academicians, and related industry professionals and provides an in-depth discussion of the latest advances.

Sarfraz begins the book with an introductory chapter on digital image processing which describes digital imaging is used widely in various real-life applications. This chapter is specifically dedicated to digital imaging history, methodologies, tasks, software, and applications.

This is followed by a chapter titled "Fast Motion Estimation's Configuration Using Diamond Pattern and ECU, CFM, and ESD Modes for Reducing HEVC Computational Complexity" by Khemiri et al., who mention that the high performance of the high-efficiency video coding (HEVC) standard makes it more suitable for high-definition resolutions. This encoding performance is coupled with tremendous encoding complexity, compared to the earlier H.264 (also referred to as advanced video coding). HEVC complexity is mainly a return to the motion estimation (ME) module that represents the important part of encoding time, which has made several researchers turn around the optimization of this module. Some researchers are interested in hardware solutions exploiting the parallel processing of field programmable gate array, graphics processing unit, or other multicore architectures, while other researchers are focused on software optimizations by inducing fast mode decision algorithms. In this context, this chapter proposes a fast HEVC encoder configuration to speed up the encoding process. Fast configuration uses different options such as early skip detection, early control unit termination, and coded block flag fast method modes. Regarding the algorithm of ME, diamond search is used in the encoding process through several video resolutions. A time saving of around 46.75% is obtained with acceptable distortion in terms of video quality and bit rate compared to the reference test model HM.16.2. This chapter can be compared to techniques in the literature for better evaluation.

Saldaña-Heredia et al., in Chapter 3, discuss "Experimental and Theoretical Investigation on the Shear Behaviour of High Strength Reinforced Concrete Beams Using Digital Image Correlation." They show that digital image processing is a useful tool that improves pictorial information for human interpretation and is mainly used for storage, transmission, and representation of different data. In this chapter, the authors introduce an optical technique that couples physical analysis with image processing for a measurement system. Optical methods have been used to obtain the stress–strain relation by different invasive and non-invasive methods, and the chapter talks about a novel non-invasive methodology to measure stress–strain evolution. The proposed technique is based upon a single laser beam reflected on a cross-section of ductile materials (steel and aluminum) while they are under a compression load. A laser beam has been measured by using Gaussian beam propagation equations. It has been proposed that the reflection area of the laser will change as the material surface area is compressed and these differences are analyzed by using digital image processing. This technique has enabled the construction of a stress–strain diagram.

The next chapter, by Tahenni and Lecompte, is on "Experimental and Theoretical Investigation on the Shear Behaviour of High Strength Reinforced Concrete Beams Using Digital Image Correlation." In this chapter, an experimental investigation is carried out on high-strength concrete (HSC) beams with and without transverse reinforcement. The beams were tested by bending under two concentrated loads using the digital image correlation technique. In the experimental device, the shear zone between the support and the loading point was digitized by a high-resolution camera. The numerical analysis of the recorded images is performed by Gom-Aramis software to obtain the deformation of concrete and to monitor the crack evolution in terms of width, spacing, and length. The different models to determine the shear capacity of reinforced concrete beams, used by the principal universal design codes such as the American ACI 318, British Standard BS 8110, European Eurocode 2, New Zealand NZS 3101, and Indian Standard IS456, have been extrapolated to HSC to evaluate the applicability of these regulations originally developed for ordinary concrete to HSC. The experimental results show that all the code models underestimate the shear contribution of HSC and at the same time greatly overestimate the transverse reinforcement contribution. Among the four models, Eurocode 2 yields the best predictions of the ultimate shear strength of HSC.

Munera et al. are motivated by an industrial approach of the use of artificial vision in Chapter 5, "Implementation of an Artificial Vision System for Welding in the

Retrofitting Process of a Robotic Arm Industrial." The authors' aim is to improve the welding process using a robotic arm; recently, this kind of robot has been associated with high-accuracy tasks like classification, welding, object manipulation, assembly, and so on. Artificial vision is not usually used in work that uses a manipulator arm; this is normally because the robot programmer plans the robot task, which is executed cyclically. However, there are some approaches where different tasks using artificial vision are implemented. This chapter proposes a retrofitting process of a manipulator welder arm Miller MR-2000. It develops an artificial vision system to be used in the positioning system. The developed system is able to look for areas suitable for the welding task between two pieces of material within a workspace; this is possible using techniques of computational vision and image processing. Subsequently, the algorithm calculates the number of welding points based on the area identified previously, and finally sends the respective coordinates by means of G code to the robot for welding the pieces.

Awareness of the problem that different search interfaces discourage patrons from using library information sources has led academic libraries to implement web-scale discovery services. These services offer the user a "Google-like" search experience of library resources. Chapter 6, "EBSCO Discovery Service (EDS) Usage in Israeli Academic Libraries," by Greenberg, is a motivation to explore library professionals' satisfaction, patrons' information behavior, and use of the EDS discovery tool service in academic libraries in Israel. Qualitative research methods through content analysis of library directors' interviews and quantitative research methods through collected library metrics (from Google analytics) data analysis regarding usage patterns and search sessions analysis have been used in this chapter.

Muhammad Sarfraz
Department of Information Science,
College of Life Sciences,
Kuwait University,
Sabah AlSalem University City,
Shadadiya,
Kuwait

Chapter 1

Introductory Chapter: On Digital Image Processing

Muhammad Sarfraz

1. Introduction

An image would be called as an analog image if its pictorial representation can be represented in analog wave formats, whereas an image would be called as a digital image if its pictorial representation can be represented or stored in the data in digital form. Similarly, field of image processing can be categorized into digital image processing and analog image processing. Digital image processing (or digital imaging), in the area of computer science today, is defined as processing digital images through some algorithms using digital computers, whereas, analog image processing is any image processing task that can be conducted on two-dimensional analog signals by analog means [1, 2].

After the invention of digital computers, digital image processing took various advantages over analog image processing. A broad range of techniques and methods, in the form of a variety of algorithms, came into existence. One can find a rich literature toady which can be applied to the input image data to solve various problems. These problems may include converting images into digital data, calibration, removing the build-up of noise and distortion during processing, etc. Since images are defined over two dimensions (and perhaps more) digital image processing may be modeled in the form of multidimensional systems. Digital image processing has evolved rapidly with the development of computers, mathematics, and the real-life demand for a variety of applications in wide range of areas [3–30].

In the current age and time, digital imaging is used widely in various real-life applications. There is a number of potential digital imaging applications that include different areas such as environment, industry, medical science, agriculture, military, film, television, photography, robotics, remote sensing, medical diagnosis, reconnaissance, architectural and engineering design, art, crime prevention, geographical information systems, communication, intellectual property, retail catalogs, nudity-detection, face finding, industrial applications, and others. The increasing trends, needs, and applications of imaging make it more difficult to process images for desired objectives. This leads to the idea of capturing, storing, finding, retrieving, analyzing, and using images in everyday life under the computing environment. Being a computer-based technology, digital imaging carries out automatic processing, manipulation, and interpretation of visual information. It plays a significant and important role in various aspects of real life. It is also highly useful in many areas, disciplines and fields of art, and science and technology. This chapter is specifically dedicated to digital imaging history, methodologies, tasks, software, and applications [31–57].

2. History

One of the earliest applications of digital image, in the early 1920s, can be seen in the newspaper industry. It was about the pictures that were sent by submarine cable between London and New York. The Bart lane cable picture transmission system reduced the amount of time tremendously weeks to hours across the Atlantic. As the field of digital image processing developed along with the development of the modern digital computers in 1950s, various techniques, methods, and technologies of digital image processing were developed in the 1960s at various places. Some of those places can be named as Bell Laboratories, the Jet Propulsion Laboratory, Massachusetts Institute of Technology, and University of Maryland. Together with them, there were also some other research facilities for satellite imagery, medical imaging, wire-photo standards conversion, photograph enhancement, videophone, and character recognition [3]. In the early days, image processing was mainly meant for improving the image quality in general. Very basic and commonly used techniques in image processing included enhancement, restoration, encoding, and compression of images.

American Jet Propulsion Laboratory (JPL) happened to be the first successful application in 1960s. Using this, in 1964, Space Detector Ranger 7 sent thousands of lunar photos. They mainly used image processing techniques like geometric correction, gradation transformation, and noise removal on the sent lunar photos. It was a big success story to have the successful computerized mapping of the moon's surface. The success kept progressing so much so that spacecraft sent nearly 100,000 photos that were processed with more complex imaging functionalities. It helped to obtain the topographic map, color map, and panoramic mosaic of the moon. This resulted in extraordinary achievements and happened to be landmark basis of history for human landing on the moon [4].

This is true that, due to computing machines of 1960s and earlier, the processing cost was fairly high. With the passage of time, in the 1970s, however, things changed relatively with faster digital image processing and cheaper computing equipment. Slowly and gradually afterwards, processing power kept increasing together with lower cost machines which resulted in images to be processed faster and faster. So much so, various complex problems like television standards conversion were managed in real time. In the years 2000s and after, the general-purpose computing equipment became much faster. Various developments in the technological world led to dedicated and special purpose hardware and equipment. Today, digital image processing has turned to a vital computing discipline which is playing a significant role to solve various real life problems in real time.

3. Methodology and tasks

Image processing is a very important area in today's science and engineering. The processing of digital images can be divided into various classes including image enhancement, image restoration, image analysis, and image compression. Imaging provides methodology to perform some kind of operations on input images. The output is obtained in terms of enhanced images, or some desired information, or some required features. For the sake of smooth workflow, it is important to first capture images and then to process them afterwards. Image processing techniques work on digital images with computing algorithms. Various steps and phases are needed to work on the images. For example, first, one can convert signals from an image sensor into digital images. After that, we can improve clarity and remove noise. Next, steps may be extracting the size, scaling, or desired objects in a scene. Then, images can be prepared for display. Lastly but not finally, compression of images is a very important phenomenon as it is needed for communication across busy networks.

There are various other phases and tasks which need attention depending on nature of applications. These include morphological processing, segmentation, enhancement, object recognition, and color image processing. Digital image processing involves much more sophisticated and useful computer algorithms. Most of the times, it is based on classification, feature extraction, multi-scale signal analysis, pattern recognition, and projection. Some of the popular techniques that can be used in digital image processing include anisotropic diffusion, Hidden Markov models, image editing, image restoration, independent component analysis, linear filtering, neural networks, partial differential equations, pixelization, point feature matching, principal components analysis, self-organizing maps, and wavelets.

4. Software and applications

There are a variety of software that can be used for image processing. For example, Matlab has many tools for image processing; it also facilitates to develop graphical user interfaces (GUI). ImageJ can be utilized for simple things, whereas Amira can be used for complex tasks. In case of medical applications, eFilm is one of the useful tools.

Applications of image processing range from medicine to entertainment and much more. Some of the important applications of image processing in the field of science, engineering, and technology include image sharpening and restoration, remote sensing, feature extraction, face detection, forecasting, optical character recognition, biometrics, medical imaging, optical sorting, augmented reality, virtual reality, video processing, microscope imaging, license plate recognition, lane departure caution, transportation, parking, transmission and encoding, machine vision, robotics, color processing, signature recognition, iris recognition, face recognition, forensics, automobile detection, fault detection, pattern recognition, military applications, and others. Following subsection has been dedicated to an application of license plate recognition (LPR) with systematic methodologies.

4.1 License plate recognition

Here is an example of different tasks and phases for a system to recognize license plates from the front and rear of the vehicle [58–60]. Input to the system is an image sequence acquired by a digital camera that consists of a license plate and its output is the recognition of characters on the license plate. The system consists of the standard four main modules in an LPR system which includes image acquisition, license plate extraction, license plate segmentation, and license plate recognition. The structure of the system is shown in **Figure 1**. The first task acquires the selected portion of the image (i.e., the portion which contains a license plate). The second task extracts the region that contains the license plate. The third task isolates the characters, consisting of letters and numerals, depending on the targeted License Plates. The last task identifies or recognizes the segmented characters.

Image acquisition: This is the first phase in an LPR system. This phase deals with acquiring an image by an acquisition method. In the LPR system, we need to use a high resolution digital camera to acquire the input image. The input image can be taken for example 640 × 480 pixels.

License plate extraction: License plate extraction is a key step in an LPR system, which influences the accuracy of the system significantly. This phase extracts the region of interest, i.e., the license plate, from the acquired image. The proposed

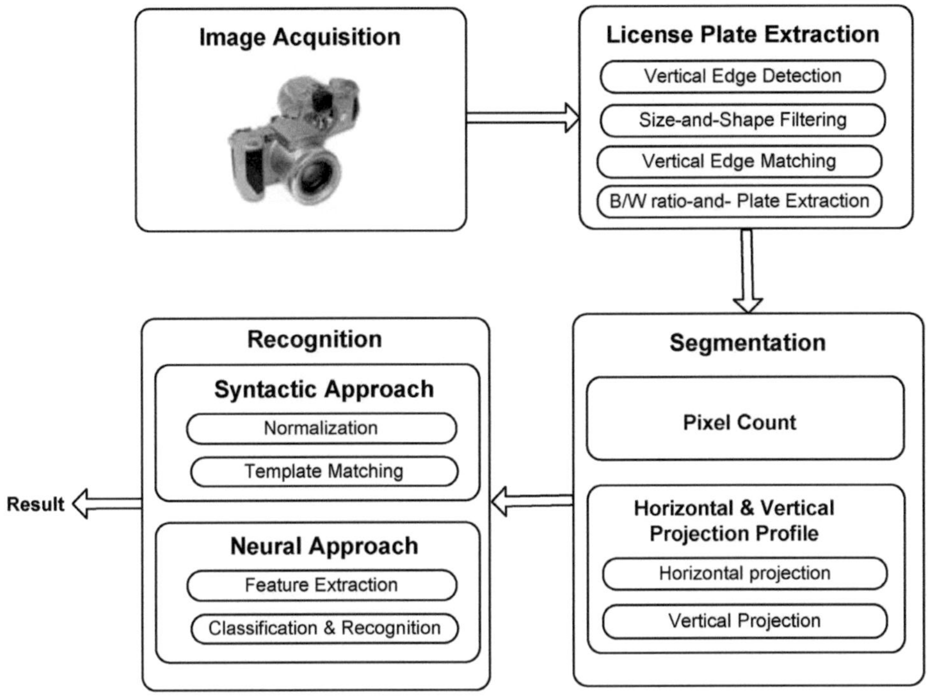

Figure 1.
Structure of the proposed system.

approach involves four steps including vertical edge detection, size-and-shape filtering, vertical edge matching, and finding B/W (Black/White) ratio.

License plate segmentation: License plate segmentation takes the region of interest and attempts to divide it into individual characters. To ease the process of detecting the characters, the extracted plate is divided into independent images, each containing one isolated character with letters and numerals depending on the structure of the license plate. It is proposed to have segmentation using two methods: Pixel Count and Horizontal and Vertical Projection.

License plate recognition: The last phase in LPR system is to recognize the isolated characters. After splitting the extracted license plate into six images, the character in each image can be identified. There are many methods to recognize isolated characters; we suggest using Syntactic approach and Neural network approach.

5. Conclusion

With the advent of fast and cheap machines, digital image processing has become a very highly demanded field of study and practice. It provides solutions to various real-life applications in an economical way. Various techniques have been developed to build intelligent systems; many of them are in progress at various facilities internationally. This chapter has provided some introductory notes on image processing, its brief history, methodologies, tasks, software, and applications. It will help to kick start the community interested to have some knowhow on the image processing subject. The future of digital image processing has a high probability to contribute toward the build of smart and intelligent world in terms of health, education, defense, traffic, homes, offices, cities, etc.

Author details

Muhammad Sarfraz
Department of Information Science, College of Life Sciences, Kuwait University, Sabah AlSalem University City, Shadadiya, Kuwait

*Address all correspondence to: prof.m.sarfraz@gmail.com; muhammad.sarfraz@ku.edu.kw

References

[1] Chakravorty P. What is a signal? [lecture notes]. IEEE Signal Processing Magazine. 2018;**35**(5):175-177. DOI: 10.1109/MSP.2018.2832195

[2] Gonzalez R. Digital image processing. New York, NY: Pearson; 2018. ISBN: 978-0-13-335672-4. OCLC 966609831

[3] Rosenfeld A. Picture Processing by Computer. New York: Academic Press; 1969

[4] Gonzalez RC, Woods RE. Digital Image Processing. 4th ed. New York, NY, USA: Pearson; 2018. ISBN-13: 978-0133356724

[5] Williams JB. The Electronics Revolution: Inventing the Future. Chichester, UK: Springer; 2017. pp. 245-248. ISBN: 9783319490885

[6] 1960: Metal Oxide Semiconductor (MOS) Transistor Demonstrated. The Silicon Engine. Computer History Museum. Archived from the original on 3 October 2019. [Accessed: 31 August 2019]

[7] Janesick JR. Scientific Charge-Coupled Devices. Bellingham, Washington, USA: SPIE Press; 2001. pp. 3-4. ISBN: 978-0-8194-3698-6

[8] Boyle WS, Smith GE. Charge coupled semiconductor devices. Bell System Technical Journal. 1970;**49**(4):587-593. DOI: 10.1002/j.1538-7305.1970.tb01790.x

[9] Fossum, Eric R. Active pixel sensors: Are CCDS dinosaurs?. In: Blouke, Morley M, editors. Charge-Coupled Devices and Solid State Optical Sensors III. Proceedings of the SPIE, 1900. Bellingham, Washington, USA: SPIE Press; 1993. pp. 2-14

[10] Fossum ER. Active Pixel Sensors. Semantic Scholar. Archived (PDF) from the original on 9 March 2019. 2007 [Accessed: 08 October 2019]

[11] Matsumoto, Kazuya, et al. A new MOS phototransistor operating in a non-destructive readout mode. Japanese Journal of Applied Physics. 1985;**24**(5A):L323. Bibcode:1985JaJAP..24L.323M. DOI: 10.1143/JJAP.24.L323

[12] Fossum ER, Hondongwa DB. A review of the pinned photodiode for CCD and CMOS image sensors. IEEE Journal of the Electron Devices Society. 2014;**2**(3):33-43. DOI: 10.1109/JEDS.2014.2306412

[13] CMOS Image Sensor Sales Stay on Record-Breaking Pace. IC Insights. 8 May 2018. Archived from the original on 21 June 2019 [Accessed: 06 October 2019]

[14] Ahmed N. How I came up with the discrete cosine transform. Digital Signal Processing. 1991;**1**(1):4-5. DOI: 10.1016/1051-2004(91)90086-Z

[15] T.81 – Digital Compression and Coding of Continuous-Tone Still Images – Requirements and Guidelines. CCITT. September 1992. Archived (PDF) from the original on 17 July 2019 [Accessed: 12 July 2019]

[16] The JPEG Image Format Explained. BT.com. BT Group. 31 May 2018. Archived from the original on 5 August 2019 [Accessed: 05 August 2019]

[17] What Is a JPEG? The Invisible Object You See Every Day. The Atlantic. 24 September 2013. Archived from the original on 9 October 2019 [Accessed: 13 September 2019]

[18] Baraniuk C. Copy protections could come to JPEGs. BBC News. BBC. Archived from the original on 9 October 2019. 2015 [Accessed: 13 September 2019]

[19] Grant DA, Gowar J. Power MOSFETS: Theory and Applications.

New York, USA: John Wiley & Sons; 1989. p. 1. ISBN: 9780471828679. The metal-oxide-semiconductor field-effect transistor (MOSFET) is the most commonly used active device in the very large-scale integration of digital integrated circuits (VLSI). During the 1970s these components revolutionized electronic signal processing, control systems and computers

[20] Shirriff K. The Surprising Story of the First Microprocessors. IEEE Spectrum. Institute of Electrical and Electronics Engineers. Archived from the original on 13 October 2019. 2016 [Accessed: 13 October 2019]

[21] 1979: Single Chip Digital Signal Processor Introduced. The Silicon Engine. Computer History Museum. Archived from the original on 3 October 2019 [Accessed: 14 October 2019]

[22] Taranovich S. 30 Years of DSP: From a Child's Toy to 4G and Beyond. EDN. Archived from the original on 14 October 2019. 2012 [Accessed: 14 October 2019]

[23] Stanković RS, Astola JT. Reminiscences of the Early Work in DCT: Interview with K. R. Rao (PDF). Reprints from the Early Days of Information Sciences. 60. Archived (PDF) from the original on 13 October 2019. 2012 [Accessed: 13 October 2019]

[24] Space Technology Hall of Fame: Inducted Technologies/1994. Space Foundation. Archived from the original on 4 July 2011. 1994 [Accessed: 07 January 2010]

[25] Zhang MZ, Livingston AR, Asari VK. A high performance architecture for implementation of 2-D convolution with quadrant symmetric kernels. International Journal of Computers and Applications. 2008;**30**(4):298-308. DOI: 10.1080/1206212x.2008.11441909

[26] Gonzalez R. Digital Image Processing. 3rd ed. New York, USA: Pearson Hall; 2008. ISBN: 9780131687288

[27] House K. Affine Transformations (PDF). Clemson. Foundations of Physically Based Modeling & Animation. A K Peters/CRC Press. ISBN: 9781482234602. Archived (PDF) from the original on 30 August 2017. 2016 [Accessed: 26 March 2019]

[28] A Brief, Early History of Computer Graphics in Film Archived 17 July 2012 at the Wayback Machine, Larry Yaeger, 16 August 2002 (last update) [Accessed: 24 March 2010]

[29] Digital Image Processing, From Wikipedia, the Free Encyclopedia [Accessed: 05 March 2020]

[30] Solomon CJ, Breckon TP. Fundamentals of Digital Image Processing: A Practical Approach with Examples in Matlab. Chichester, UK: Wiley-Blackwell; 2010

[31] Burger W, Burge MJ. Digital Image Processing: An Algorithmic Approach Using Java. London, UK: Springer; 2007. ISBN: 978-1-84628-379-6

[32] Fisher R, Dawson-Howe K, Fitzgibbon A, Robertson C, Trucco E. Dictionary of Computer Vision and Image Processing. Chichester, UK: John Wiley; 2005. ISBN: 978-0-470-01526-1

[33] Gonzalez RC, Woods RE, Eddins SL. Digital Image Processing Using MATLAB. India: Pearson Education; 2004. ISBN: 978-81-7758-898-9

[34] Morris T. Computer Vision and Image Processing. New York, USA: Palgrave Macmillan; 2004. ISBN: 978-0-333-99451-1

[35] Sonka M, Hlavac V, Boyle R. Image Processing, Analysis, and Machine Vision. Pacific Grove, CA, USA: PWS Publishing; 1999. ISBN: 978-0-534-95393-5

[36] Gonzalez RC. Digital Image Processing. New York, USA: Prentice Hall; 2008. ISBN: 9780131687288

[37] Ebad Banissi, Anna Ursyn, Autilia Vitiello, Fatma Bouali, Gilles Venturin, Hanane Azzag, et al. Information Visualization - Biomedical Visualization, Visualisation on Built and Rural Environments & Geometric Modelling and Imaging. USA: IEEE Computer Society. 2019

[38] Banissi E, Francese R, McK Bannatyne MW, Wyeld TG, Sarfraz M, Pires JM, et al, editors. Information Visualization - Biomedical Visualization, Visualisation on Built and Rural Environments & Geometric Modellinpg and Imaging. USA: IEEE Computer Society; 2018

[39] Banissi E, McK Bannatyne MW, Bouali F, Datia NMS, Grinstein G, et al, editors. Information Visualization - Biomedical Visualization, Visualisation on Built and Rural Environments & Geometric Modelling and Imaging, IEETe 2017. USA: IEEE Computer Society; 2017

[40] Banissi E, Sarfraz M, Zeroul A, Fakir M, editors. Computer Graphics, Imaging & Visualization. New Horizons, USA: IEEE; 2017

[41] Banissi E, Pires JM, McK MW, Bannatyne UC, Grinstein G, Huang T, et al, editors. Information Visualization - Biomedical Visualization, Visualisation on Built and Rural Environments & Geometric Modelling and Imaging. USA: IEEE Computer Society; 2016

[42] Banissi E, Sarfraz M, Fakir M, editors. Computer Graphics, Imaging & Visualization: New Techniques and Trends. USA: IEEE; 2016

[43] Banissi E, Sarfraz M, editors. Computer Graphics, Imaging & Visualization: New Techniques and Trends. USA: IEEE; 2015

[44] Banissi E, McK Bannatyne MW, Marchese FT, Wyeld TG, Sarfraz M, Ursyn A, et al, editors. Information Visualisation - Computer Graphics, Imaging and Visualisation: Biomedical Visualization, Visualisation on Built and Rural Environments & Geometric Modelling and Imaging. USA: IEEE Computer Society; 2015

[45] Sarfraz M. Computer Vision and Image Processing in Intelligent Systems and Multimedia Technologies. Hershey, PA: IGI Global; 2014. pp. 1-312

[46] Banissi E, Sarfraz M. Computer Graphics, Imaging & Visualization: New Techniques and Trends. USA: IEEE; 2014

[47] Banissi E, McK Bannatyne MW, Marchese FT, Sarfraz M, Ursyn A, Venturini G, et al. Information Visualization: Visualisation, BioMedical Visualization, Visualisation on Built and Rural Environments & Geometric Modelling and Imaging. USA: IEEE; 2014

[48] Sarfraz M. Interactive Curve Modeling with Applications to Computer Graphics, Vision and Image Processing. London, UK: Springer-Verlag; 2008

[49] Saad A, Avineri E, Dahal K, Sarfraz M, Roy R. Soft Computing in Industrial Applications: Recent and Emerging Methods and Techniques, Series: Advances in Soft Computing, Vol. 39. London, UK: Springer- Verlag; 2007

[50] Sarfraz M. Computer Aided Intelligent Recognition Techniques and Applications. Chichester, UK: John Wiley and Sons; 2005

[51] Khalloufi R, El Ayachi R, Biniz M, Fakir M, Sarfraz M. An approach of documents indexing using summarization. In: Sarfraz M, editor. Critical Approaches to Information

Retrieval Research. Hershey, PA: IGI Global; 2020. pp. 78-86

[52] Taifi K, Taifi N, Fakir M, Safi S, Sarfraz M. Mammogram classification using nonsubsampled contourlet transform and gray-level co-occurrence matrix. In: Sarfraz M, editor. Critical Approaches to Information Retrieval Research. Hershey, PA: IGI Global; 2020. pp. 239-255

[53] Fakir M, Hicham H, Chabi M, Sarfraz M. Classification of eye based on fuzzy logic. International Journal of Cognitive Informatics and Natural Intelligence. 2020;**14**(4):1-20

[54] Ebrahimi AR, Loghmani GB, Sarfraz M. Capturing outlines of generic shapes with cubic B'ezier curves using the Nelder–Mead simplex method. Iranian Journal of Numerical Analysis and Optimization. 2019;**9**(2):103-121. DOI: 10.22067/ijnao.v9i2.70045

[55] Zulkifli NAB, Karim SAA, Shafie AB, Sarfraz M. Rational bicubic ball for image interpolation. Journal of Physics: Conference Series. 2019;**1366**(1):1-11. DOI: 10.1088/1742-6596/1366/1/012097

[56] Zulkifli NAB, Karim SAA, Shafie AB, Sarfraz M, Gaffar A, Nisar KS. Image interpolation using rational bi-cubic ball. Mathematics. 2019;**7**(11):1-18. DOI: 10.3390/math7111045

[57] Essays UK. The History of Image Processing Information Technology Essay. 2013. Available from: https://www.uniassignment.com/essay-samples/information-technology/the-history-of-image-processing-information-technology-essay.php?vref=1

[58] Yusuf AS, Sarfraz M. Color Edge Enhancement Based Fuzzy Segmentation of License Plates, the Proceedings of IEEE International Conference on Information Visualisation (IV'2005)-UK. Los Alamitos, USA: IEEE Computer Society Press; 2005. 991-996

[59] Ahmed MJ, Sarfraz M, Zidouri A, Alkhatib WG. License Plate Recognition System, the Proceedings of the 10th IEEE International Conference on Electronics, Circuits and Systems (ICECS2003). Sharjah, United Arab Emirates (UAE): IEEE; 2003

[60] Sarfraz M, Ahmed M, Ghazi SA. Saudi Arabian License Plate Recognition System, the Proceedings of IEEE International Conference on Geoemetric Modeling and Graphics-GMAG'2003-UK. USA: IEEE Computer Society Press; 2003

Chapter 2

Fast Motion Estimation's Configuration Using Diamond Pattern and ECU, CFM, and ESD Modes for Reducing HEVC Computational Complexity

Randa Khemiri, Nejmeddine Bahri, Fatma Belghith, Soulef Bouaafia, Fatma Elzahra Sayadi, Mohamed Atri and Nouri Masmoudi

Abstract

The high performance of the high efficiency video coding (HEVC) video standard makes it more suitable for high-definition resolutions. Nevertheless, this encoding performance is coupled with a tremendous encoding complexity compared to the earlier H264 video codec. The HEVC complexity is mainly a return to the motion estimation (ME) module that represents the important part of encoding time which makes several researches turn around the optimization of this module. Some works are interested in hardware solutions exploiting the parallel processing of FPGA, GPU, or other multicore architectures, and other works are focused on software optimizations by inducing fast mode decision algorithms. In this context, this article proposes a fast HEVC encoder configuration to speed up the encoding process. The fast configuration uses different options such as the early skip detection (ESD), the early CU termination (ECU), and the coded block flag (CBF) fast method (CFM) modes. Regarding the algorithm of ME, the diamond search (DS) is used in the encoding process through several video resolutions. A time saving around 46.75% is obtained with an acceptable distortion in terms of video quality and bitrate compared to the reference test model HM.16.2. Our contribution is compared to other works for better evaluation.

Keywords: HEVC, motion estimation, early skip detection (ESD), early CU termination (ECU), coded block flag (CBF) fast method (CFM)

1. Introduction

The fast multimedia technology development and network communications makes ultrahigh-definition (HD) and HD video contents widely used in our daily life. This fast jump to use high video resolutions in which many provide some problems in terms of memory storage cost and transmission bandwidth gives birth

IntechOpen

to the new high efficiency video coding (HEVC) [1, 2]. HEVC is developed in 2013 by the joint collaborative team on video coding (ISO/IEC) Moving Picture Experts Group (MPEG) and the International ITU-T Video Coding Experts Group (VCEG). It is urbanized to overcome the enormous amount of UHD video contents. Compared to the earlier H.264/AVC [3] standard and at the identical visual quality, HEVC guarantees a high encoding performance, reaching 50% of bitrate [4]. Facing to this immense huge encoding performance, a huge computational complexity is obtained. Motion estimation (ME) represents the large part of encoding process that occupies around 70% of the total time of inter prediction, as Jungho [5] indicates in **Figure 1**.

This large consumption is principally due to the new hierarchy of the block coding based on coding tree units (CTU). This new concept is analog to macroblocks in the earlier standard of compression. Each picture frame is divided into square forms, called coding units (CUs) [6], where 64 × 64 represents the maximum size, and recursively subdivided into 8 × 8 blocks. Prediction and

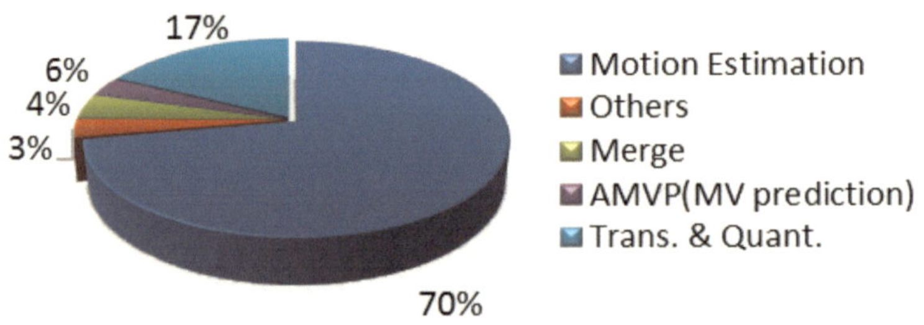

Figure 1.
Encoding time distribution.

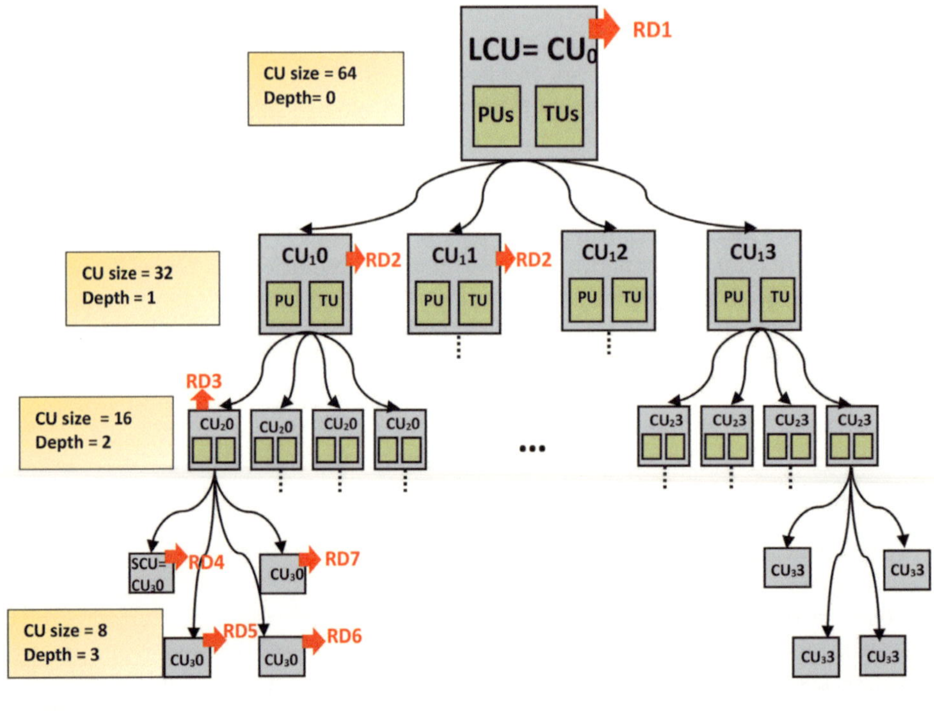

Figure 2.
CTU tree structure in the HEVC standard.

transform blocks (PUs and TUs) are in each CU, where PU represents the principal unit in the ME process.

Figure 2 shows the CTU tree structure in the HEVC standard where LCU represents the large coding unit and SCU represents the small coding unit.

When reducing the time essential for the search algorithm, the ME computational complexity will be automatically reduced. Furthermore, when using different fast mode decision algorithms based on early termination, the ME computational complexity will be reduced, which primes to the entire HEVC execution time reduction.

It is within this context that this article presents a fast encoding algorithm principally based on the early skip detection (ESD), the coded block flag (CBF) fast method (CFM), and the early CU termination (ECU) modes [7–9] to decrease the HEVC encoding complexity.

The remainder of this paper is structured as follows: the next section details some works on the HEVC fast motion estimation algorithms. Section 3 provided an overview of the motion estimation algorithm. Section 4 highlights the proposed fast configuration for the HEVC encoder. Experimental results for the fast HEVC configuration compared to the results obtained with the original HM16.2 reference software [10] are discussed in Section 5. Finally, in Section 6, conclusions and some prospects are given.

2. Related works

Aiming to optimize the HEVC encoder complexity, several works have been proposed to reduce the test zonal search (TZS) motion estimation algorithm. Some works are interested in hardware solutions, and others are focused on software optimizations.

In [11], using sequential and parallel techniques, two hardware diamond architectures for HEVC video coding are proposed. These architectures achieve an encoding in full HD at 30 frames per second using a Virtex-7 field programmable gate array (FPGA) design.

Authors in [12] have proposed a hardware parallel sum of absolute difference (SAD) design for gray-scale images to reduce motion estimation time for block size of 4×4 pixels. A multiplier is exploited for addition as a partial product reduction (PPR). Results obtained on Virtex-2 Xilinx FPGA show that the maximum frequency obtained is 133.2 MHz for 4×4 block size. Nalluri et al., in [13, 14], have proposed two other SAD architectures on FPGA Xilinx Virtex without and with parallelism. The proposed parallel architecture has accelerated the SAD calculation by 3.9× compared to the serial SAD architecture. In [15], authors have proposed two implementations of the SAD and SSD algorithms using NVIDIA GeForce GTX480 with CUDA language in order to reduce the ME run-time. The proposed architecture saved about 32% of encoding time for class E video sequences with nonsignificant degradation in the PSNR and the bitrate.

Regarding software solutions, the 8-point square and the 8-point diamond have been replaced by Nalluri et al. [16] with a 6-point hexagonal in the TZS ME algorithm, and 50% in encoding time is saved without degradation in bitrate and PSNR. To replace the TZS algorithm, in [17, 18], authors proposed small diamond pattern search (SDPS), large diamond pattern search (LDPS), and horizontal diamond search (HDS). Experiments using HM8.0 showed that these algorithms allow a reduction of 49% of motion estimation calculation time with nonsignificant increase in bitrate and slight degradation in video quality.

In [19], Liquan et al. have proposed a fast mode decision algorithm by skipping some depths. The proposed work allows saving about 21.5% of encoding time with a slight bitrate increase and a negligible efficiency loss coding. The algorithm proposed by Qin [20] uses the ECU algorithm according to an adaptive MSE threshold value. This work ensures time saving without degradation in the quality. Podder [21] has also proposed an interesting software method to reduce the ME time. Based on human visual features (HVF), an efficient decision of the appropriate block partitioning mode has been obtained. This work allows saving 41.44% of the execution time for SCVS video sequences. In the work published in [22], a fast HEVC ME based on DS and three fast mode decisions, ECU, ESD, and CBF modes, have been presented. Simulation results show a reduction of 56.75% in the complexity of HEVC in terms of execution time, accompanied with slight degradation in video quality and bitrate, when comparing the HM.16.2 executed on an Intel® Core TM i7–3770 @3.4 GHz processor. Authors in [22] have tested just one sequence from each class with just two quantification parameters (QPs), QP = 22 and 37, to evaluate the use of the fast modes.

By analyzing all these previous works, we can note that using fast mode decision algorithms represents an interesting technique in order to reduce the HEVC computational complexity.

3. Overview of the motion estimation in the new HEVC

TZ Search algorithm, used in HEVC ME process (**Figure 3**), includes four distinct main stages in order to determine the best motion vector.

These stages, which are the motion vector prediction (MVP), the first search performed with a pattern of square or diamond forms, the refinement, and the raster search, are described in the next subsections.

3.1 Motion vector prediction (MVP)

To compute the corresponding block's median predictor, the TZS algorithm uses the up predictor, the upper right predictor, and the left predictor (**Figure 4**).

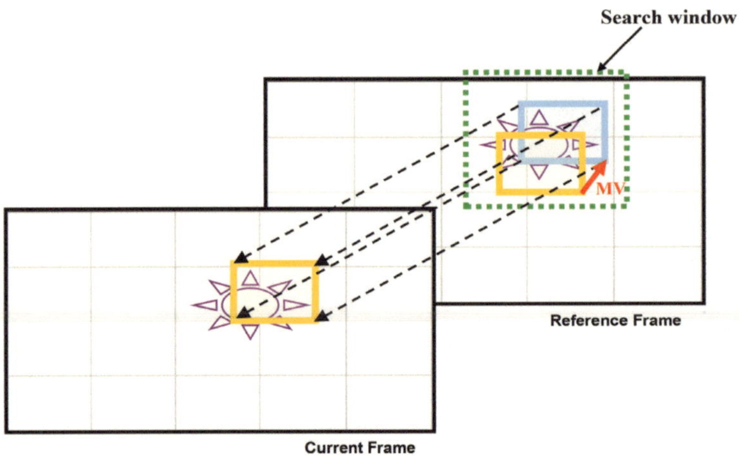

Figure 3.
Motion estimation process.

The median computation is done via the following equation.

$$Median(A, B, C) = A + B + C - \mathrm{Min}(A, \mathrm{Min}(B, C)) - \mathrm{Max}(A, \mathrm{Max}(B, C)) \quad (1)$$

3.2 Initial grid search

The first search is performed by the determination of the search pattern and the "searchrange." As it is detailed in **Figure 5(a)** and **(b)**, the main goal of this stage is to localize the search window via a pattern of square or a diamond forms.

Thus, these two search patterns are referred to the eight points for each round. The distance corresponding to the minimum distortion point is saved in the "BestDistance" variable. Currently, diamond search pattern is used as default, but the square pattern search can also be used by modifying the HEVC configuration file through the "Diamondsearch" variable.

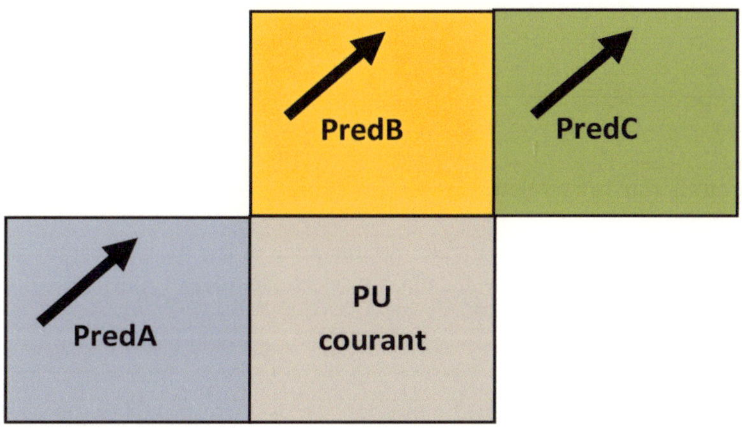

Figure 4.
MV adjacent of a current PU.

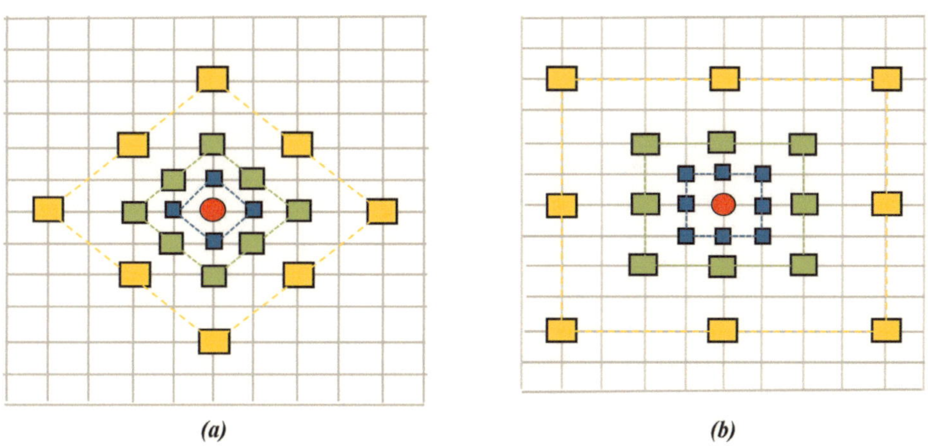

Figure 5.
Diamond/square search pattern. (a) Diamond search pattern stride length equal to 4. (b) Square search pattern stride length equal to 4.

3.3 Raster search

This step consists of choosing the distance which corresponds to the greatest matched point from the previous search. Three cases according to this distance denoted as "BestDistance" are summarized as follows:

- The process is stopped when "BestDistance" = 0.

- A refinement is needed when 1 < "BestDistance" < iRaster.

In the configuration file, "iRaster" represents a changeable variable not to be overdone.

- BestDistance > iRaster is agreed correctly; a raster scan is achieved using the iRaster value as the length step. If difference obtained from the starting station to the MV from the first level is besides large, this step is preceded. This step is computed on the entire search window.

Figure 6 shows an example of a full search algorithm with iRaster which is equal to 4.

3.4 Raster and star refinement

The refinement is performed when the distance of the motion vector previously obtained is different to 0. There are mainly two refinement types:

- Raster refinement

The best point obtained from the previous steps corresponds to the start point of the star refinement. It can be performed using a diamond or a square pattern with distances ranging from "search range" to one. In each iteration, the distance is divided by 2, and when the distance will be equal to one, two adjacent point searches are performed, and then the process is stopped.

- Star refinement

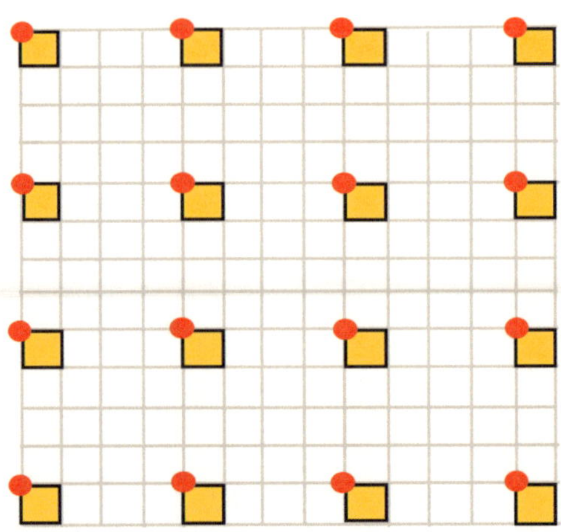

Figure 6.
Raster search pattern when iRaster = 4.

In this step, the selected point obtained from the previous steps corresponds to the start point of the star refinement. In each iteration, the distance is divided by two, and when the distance will be equal to one, two adjacent point searches are

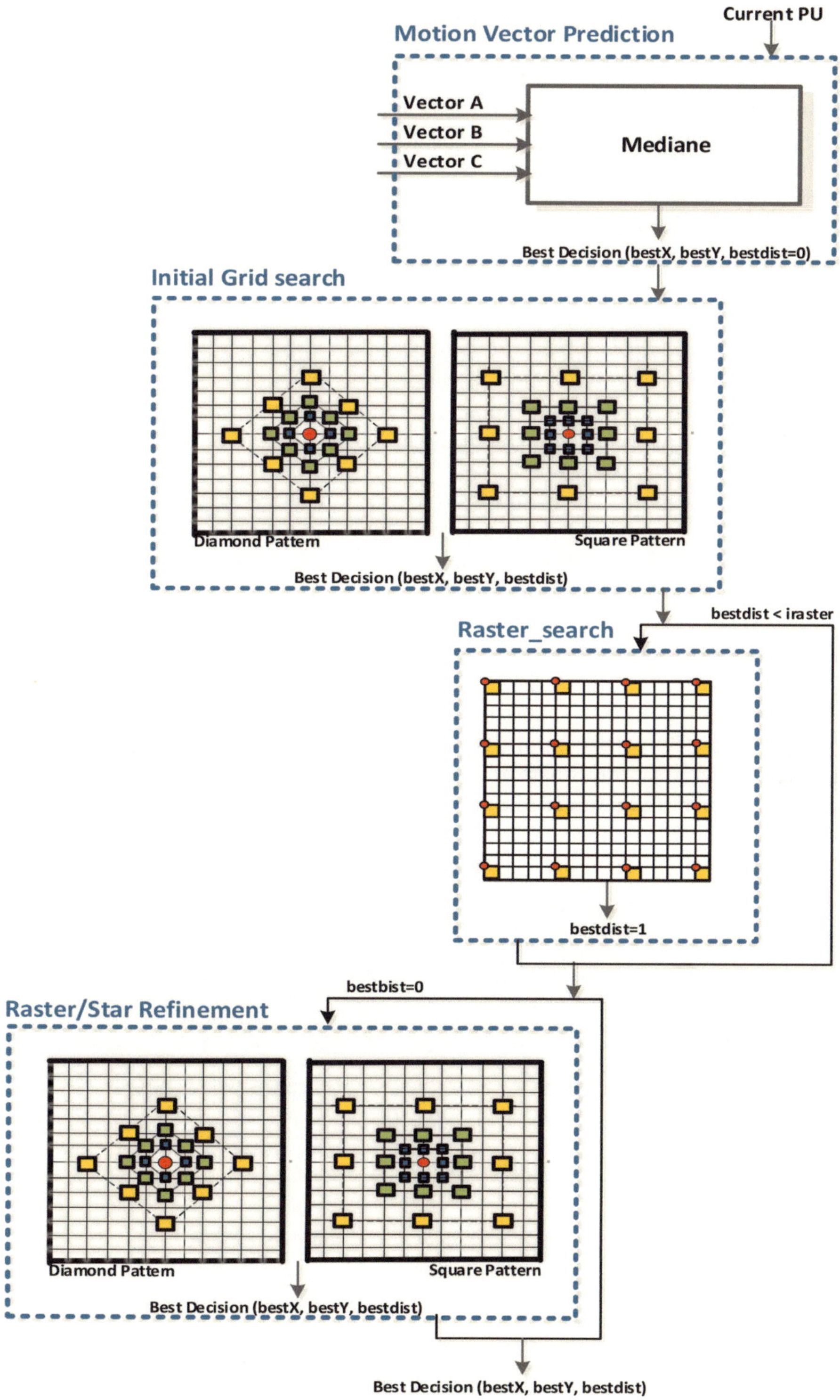

Figure 7.
The used TZSearch algorithm.

applied to determine the best estimated MV which gives the minimum of SAD (**Figure 7**).

4. The proposed fast configuration

Several fast decision mode algorithms are in this effort aiming to speed up the ME process. Firstly, diamond search pattern is utilized to decrease the encoder computational complexity. Some configurations are also set, such as the early CU termination (ECU), the early skip detection (ESD), and the coded block flag (CBF) in which fast decision mode algorithms are adopted in HEVC video coding. These proposed fast algorithms were given bellow.

4.1 Early CU termination (ECU)

This algorithm is used when switching from a depth p to the next p + 1. As **Figure 8** showed, if skip is the best current CU prediction mode, the sub-tree calculations can be skipped [23]. Thus, good mode is determined with rate distortion (RD) calculation cost [24]. The minimal RD cost relates to the skip mode that caused the stop of the partitioning [25].

Several works show that the most chosen mode was the skip [25]. This clarifies the detail that an excessive enhancement is obtained when the skip mode recognition is anticipated. This mode induces a better encoder performance since it denotes a block code deprived of residual information.

4.2 Early skip detection (ESD)

The early skip detection signifies a modest verification of the two-variance motion skip conditions (CBF and differential motion vector (DMV)). As shown in **Figure 9**, this verification is performed after determining the best inter $2\,N \times 2\,N$. Before checking the skip mode, the current CU performs two inter $2\,N \times 2\,N$ modes

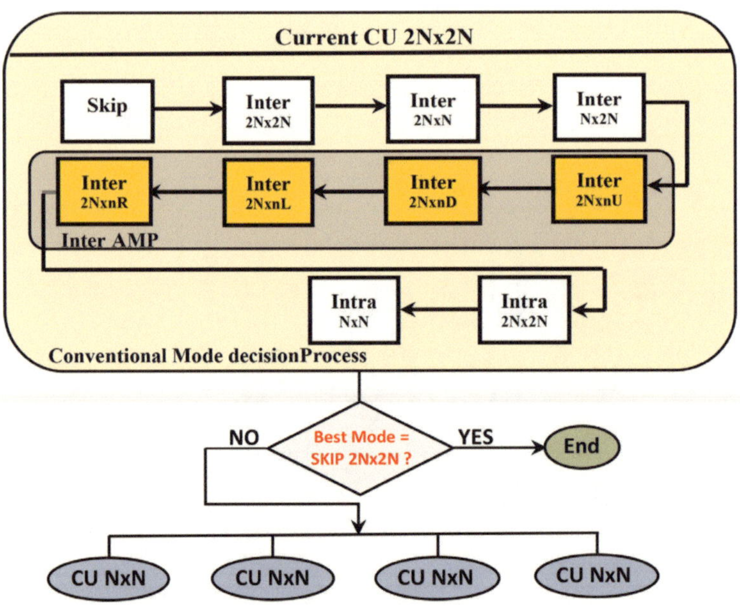

Figure 8.
Algorithm of early CU termination.

(advanced motion vector prediction called AMVP and merge mode). The DMV and CBF are checked when the minimum RD cost is induced by the mode selection. When CBF is equivalent to zero and the best mode inter 2 N × 2 N DMV is equal to (0, 0), the skip mode is the best mode of current CU. Consequently, the residual modes of PU are not examined anymore [8].

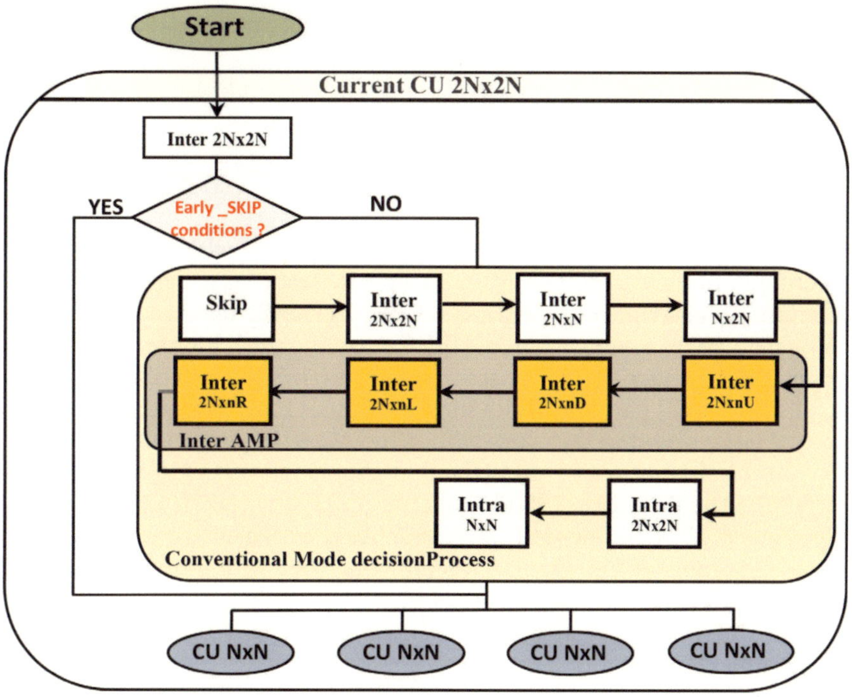

Figure 9.
Early skip detection algorithm.

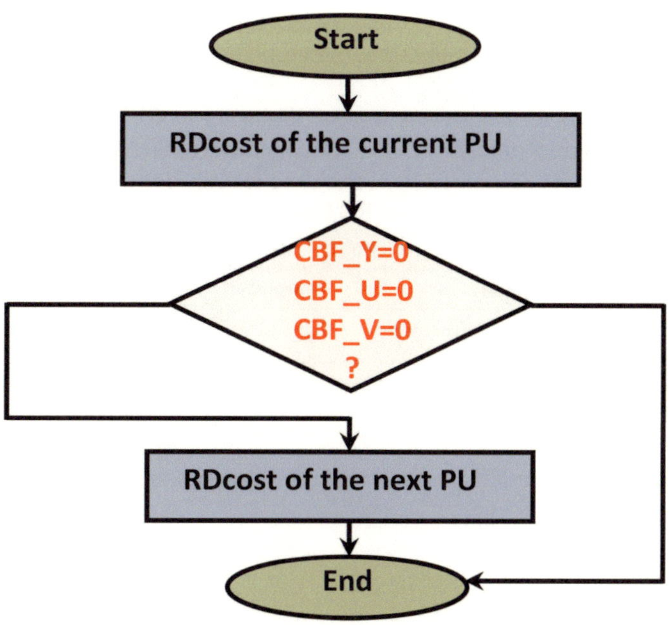

Figure 10.
Algorithm of coded block flag fast method.

4.3 Coded fast method (CFM)

The coded fast method (CFM) detects the best mode of a prediction unit [7]. As shown in **Figure 10**, for each PU mode belonging to a CU, the RD cost is calculated.

An evaluation of the different coefficients, CBF for the luminance and the two chrominances, is performed. When all transform coefficients (CBF_Y, CBF_U, and CBF_V) are equal to zero [9], all remaining modes will not be tested.

5. Experimental results

5.1 Experimental conditions

The performance evaluation of this work is effectuated with a random access (RA) configuration through the HM 16.2 reference test model, exploiting the fast mode decision algorithms ECU, ESD, and CBF, previously detailed. To appraise the fast implementation, a comparison of HEVC encoding time, bitrate, and PSNR with the original is effectuated, where a search range is 64. Sixty-four also is the CU maximal size and CU partition depth maximal equals four. An Intel® Core TM i7–3770 @ 3.4 GHz is used in this work with Windows 8 OS platform.

The four resolutions tested are to the four classes (class D (416 × 240), class C (832 × 480), class B (1920 × 1080), and class A (2560 × 1600)) [26]. For each video sequence, 50 is the encoded frame number used. To evaluate results, eight sequences recommended by the JCT-VC [26], each one with four quantification parameters (QP) 22, 27, 32, and 37, are used.

5.2 Evaluation criteria

To evaluate this work, we used the formula detailed in **Table 1**.

5.3 Results

Table 2 specifies the results obtained when using the proposed fast HEVC configuration compared to the original one.

The proposed algorithm shows a time saving of up to 46.759% on average compared to the original algorithm. The speedup attains 84.51% of encoding time for BQTerrace video for QP 37. In fact, the time saving is more important for some videos such as Traffic, BQSquare, and BQTerrace sequences ranging from 57.91 to

Criteria	Description	Formula
ΔT (%)	Encoding time speedup	$\Delta T(\%) = \frac{T_{Proposed} - T_{Original}}{T_{Original}} \times 100\ (\%)$
ΔPSNR (dB)	PSNR loss	$\Delta PSNR = \text{PSNR}_{Proposed} - \text{PSNR}_{Original}\ (\text{dB})$
ΔBR (%)	Bitrate increase	$\Delta BR(\%) = \frac{BitRate_{Proposed} - BitRate_{Original}}{BitRate_{Original}} \times 100(\%)$

Where: $Bitrate_{original}$, $PSNR_{original}$ and $T_{original}$ represent bitrate, video quality, and encoding time of the original algorithm, respectively and $Bitrate_{proposed}$, $PSNR_{proposed}$ and $T_{proposed}$, $BitRate_{Proposed}$ represent bitrate, video quality, and encoding time of the proposed algorithm, respectively.

Table 1.
Evaluation criteria.

Class	Sequences	QP	ΔT(%)	ΔPSNR (dB)	ΔBR(%)
Class A 2560 × 1600	PeopleOnStreet	22	−25.04	−0.040	−0.470
		27	−28.37	−0.100	−0.006
		32	−39.44	−0.187	−1.086
		37	−49.69	−0.030	−2.182
	Traffic	22	−47.27	−0.103	−0.018
		27	−62.04	−0.128	−0.017
		32	−71.83	−0.180	−0.027
		37	−79.40	−0.194	−0.024
Average class A			**−50.385**	**−0.123**	**−0.478**
Class B 1920 × 1080	BQTerrace	22	−29.91	−0.060	−1.180
		27	−60.27	−0.086	−0.022
		32	−76.67	−0.081	−0.021
		37	−84.51	−0.067	−2.000
	BasketballDrive	22	−32.15	−0.015	−0.004
		27	−45.23	−0.026	−0.157
		32	−54.85	−0.059	−0.640
		37	−63.82	−0.084	−0.009
Average class B			**−55.926**	**−0.059**	**−0.504**
Class C 832 × 480	RaceHorses	22	−11.45	−0.029	−1.430
		27	−22.79	−0.073	−0.005
		32	−35.24	−0.166	−0.010
		37	−44.10	−0.230	−2.138
	PartyScene	22	−19.90	−0.040	−0.002
		27	−35.13	−0.115	−0.009
		32	−47.93	−0.168	−0.016
		37	−58.59	−0.194	−0.027
Average class C			**−34.400**	**−0.126**	**−0.454**
Class D 416 × 240	BQSquare	22	−34.64	−0.075	−0.870
		27	−54.78	−0.137	−0.016
		32	−66.90	−0.156	−0.012
		37	−75.35	−0.137	−0.810
	BlowingBubbles	22	−17.81	−0.070	−0.005
		27	−28.62	−0.110	−0.005
		32	−40.05	−0.134	−0.015
		37	−52.46	−0.115	−0.012
Average class D			**−46.326**	**−0.116**	**−0.218**
Average			**−46.759**	**−0.106**	**−0.416**

Table 2.
Performance evaluation of the proposed algorithm compared to the original one.

65.135%. This is due to the motion slowness in these sequences. Indeed, for videos containing low motion activities [18], the improvement is more significant. With the highest resolution, traffic video is characterized by intensive movement of objects against a stationary background. Concerning BQSquare, this video having fast motion is often coded by the bi-predictive mode, as it is the best prediction mode.

Defiantly for sequences with high activity, such as BlowingBubbles, RaceHorses, and PeopleOnStreet, the time saving is only around 34.73 and 28.38%. The worst case is for the motion-filled and dynamic RaceHorses video, which records horse

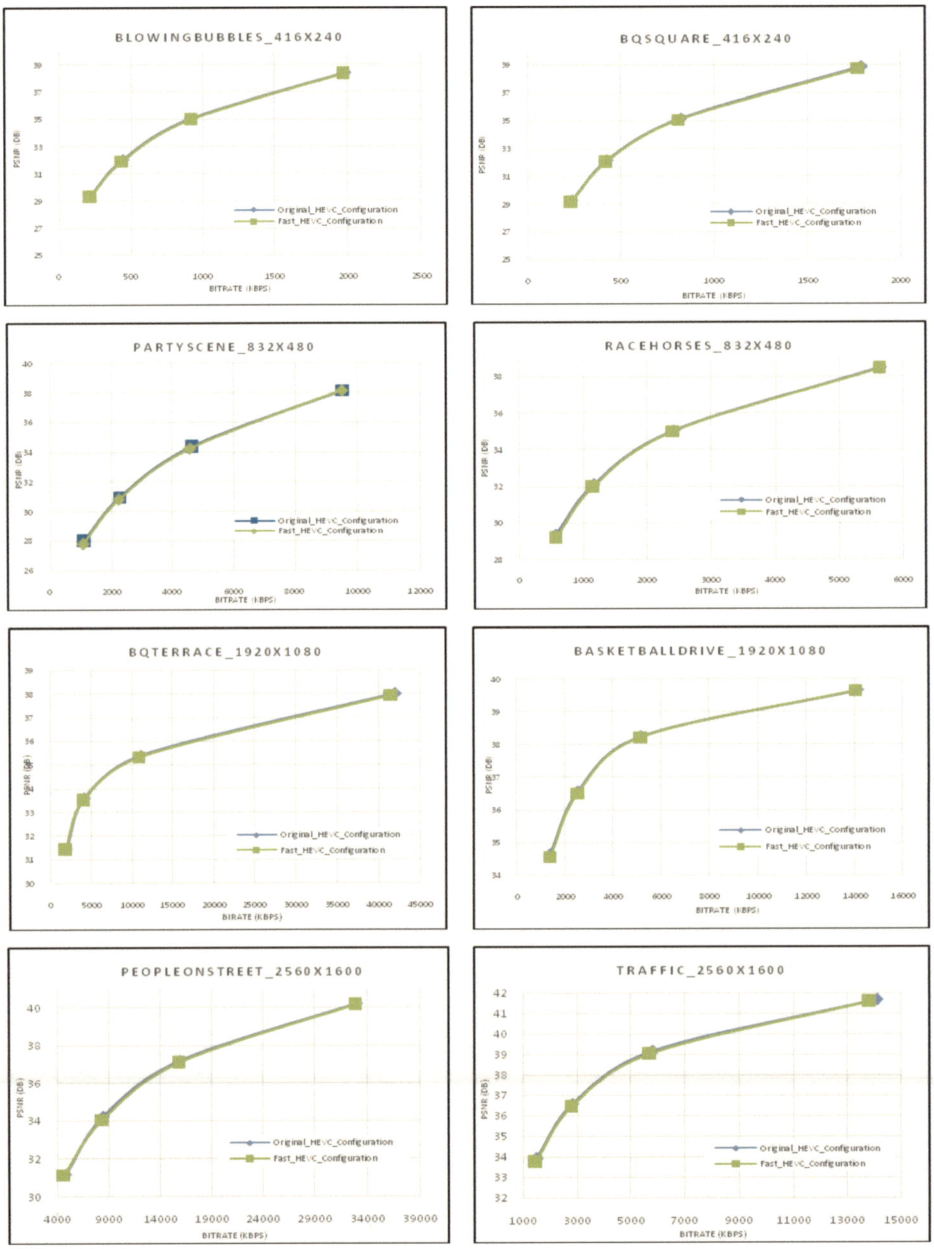

Figure 11.
RD curve comparison of our algorithm versus the original one.

racing. Many great frequency details are in this video, since horsetail is regularly expensive to encode.

The time saving is visible with 49% for BasketballDrive sequence. This video contains a high contrast and high motion activities. The background has a rather similar texture.

Not only the encoding time was saved but also the bitrate which is justified by the negative values in the table, ranging from 0.002 to −2.182% for PartyScene and PeopleOnStreet with QP equal to 22 and 37, respectively. Regarding the quality of video, the PSNR deprivation is from −0.015 to −0.23 dB for BasketballDrive and RaceHorses with QP equal to 22 and 37, respectively.

In average, the fast HEVC configuration induces a nonsignificant poverty in terms of video quality, around 0.106 dB, with a decrease of 0.416% in the bitrate that is a very interesting point in terms of increasing the compression performance.

Figure 11 shows the curves of rate distortion (RD) of HEVC original algorithm and the fast one, for two sequences for each class: PeopleOnStreet and Traffic from class A (2560 × 1600), BQTerrace and BasketballDrive from class B (1920 × 1080), PartyScene and BasketballDrive from class C (832 × 480), and BlowingBubbles and BQSquare from class D (416 × 240). This can also be checked in **Table 2**. The sequences are taken at QPs 22, 27, 32, and 37.

Four QP parameters are presented in all curves; horizontal axes on (kbps) represent the bitrate where the vertical one on (dB) represents the PSNR.

Figure 11 shows that all RD curves are overlaid [27]. In fact, the proposed changes have insignificant impairments on bitrate and PSNR. For lower QP values, the degradation is more significant. Experimental results prove that the fast configuration gives better performances than the original one, given that it offers a significant time saving, without any influence on the quality and the bitrate.

Further, for all tested sequences, an important speedup is obtained for bigger QPs. **Figure 12** evaluates the time saving in average by varying from 22 to 37. We note that the time saving increases in proportion to QP. In average, for higher QP, equal to 37, the run-time decreases by 63.5%. This decline is justified by the choice of the skip mode for bigger QP values [25].

Table 3 summarizes the performances of the proposed work compared to different previous algorithms.

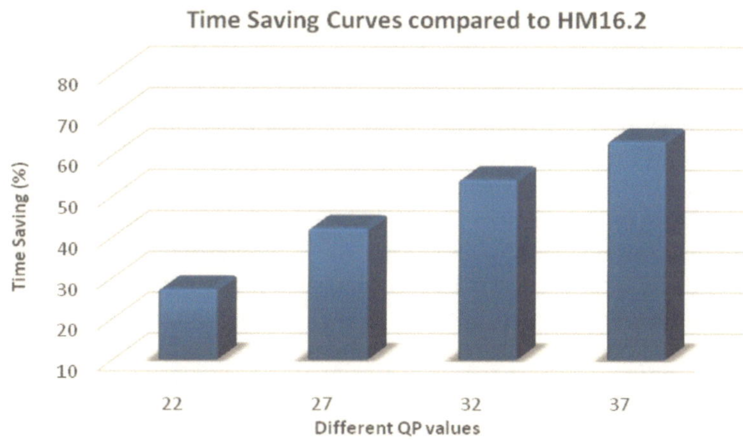

Figure 12.
Curves of time saving for all videos coded through random access configuration with QP from 22 to 37.

	Kibeya [17]			Liquan [19]			Qin [20]		
	ΔPSNR (dB)	**ΔBR (%)**	**ΔT (%)**	**ΔPSNR (dB)**	**ΔBR (%)**	**ΔT (%)**	**ΔPSNR (dB)**	**ΔBR (%)**	**ΔT (%)**
Class A	−0.052	1.08	30.67	—	—	—	0.1%	—	−22.4
Class B	−0.013	0.29	45.37	−0.020	0.834	−34.00	0.3%	—	−28.4
Class C	−0.011	0.53	20.86	−0.045	1.225	−16.50	0.2%	—	−23.0
Class D	−0.008	0.26	6.9	−0.040	1.060	−13. 50	0.2%	—	−17.0
Average	−0.0105	0.54	25.95	−0.035	1.039	−21.33	0.2%	—	−22.7

	Podder [21]			Proposed fast algorithm		
	ΔPSNR (dB)	**ΔBR (%)**	**ΔT (%)**	**ΔPSNR (dB)**	**ΔBR (%)**	**ΔT (%)**
Class A	—	—	−41.9	−0.123	−0.478	−50.384
Class B	—	—	−34.37	−0.059	−0.504	−55.926
Class C	—	—	−42.92	−0.126	−0.454	−34.400
Class D	—	—	−46.57	−0.116	−0.218	−46.326
Average	—	—	−41.44	−0.106	−0.416	−46.759

Table 3.
Proposed algorithm compared to previous works.

Compared to [17], the proposed work was more competent in terms of bitrate and saving time. In fact, [17] allows saving about 25.95% of encoding time with a slight bitrate. This algorithm was based on large diamond search pattern as an algorithm for motion estimation implemented on HM8.0. Concerning Liquan [19], its algorithm consists of skipping some detailed depths used in the preceding frames. This work allows saving about 21.5% of encoding time with a slight bitrate. Qin [20] implemented an algorithm established on the ECU according to a MSE adaptive threshold value. A time saving without degradation in the quality is obtained in this work. Another interesting method was presented by Podder et al. [21], where human visual features (HVF) are used for the selection of appropriate block partitioning modes. This work offered 41.44% reduction in terms of time for the standard class video sequences (SCVS).

6. Conclusion

HEVC induces an important progress in terms of video quality, in particular for high video resolutions. Nevertheless, this recital is combined with a bigger computational complexity which tremendously increases the encoding time. Motion estimation module using the quadtree structure represents the mainly strong process that is a conduit to the augmentation of the HEVC computational complication. In this paper to decrease this computational complexity, one fast configuration was presented to optimize the ME process by using CU partitioning fast mode decision algorithm and a diamond search. A reduction of 46.75% in the encoding time is obtained without inducing a significant degradation in encoding performance in terms of video quality or bitrate.

As perspectives, additional optimizations will be also implemented to reduce the encoder complexity via digital platform for video processing.

We will also exploit the fast configuration detailed in this paper for the new compression standard Joint Video Exploration Team (JVET) [28, 29].

Author details

Randa Khemiri[1*], Nejmeddine Bahri[2], Fatma Belghith[2], Soulef Bouaafia[1], Fatma Elzahra Sayadi[1], Mohamed Atri[1] and Nouri Masmoudi[2]

1 Electronics and Microelectronics Laboratory, Monastir University, Faculty of Sciences of Monastir, Monastir, Tunisia

2 Laboratory of Electronics and Information Technology, National Engineering School of Sfax, Sfax University, Tunisia

*Address all correspondence to: randa.khemiri@gmail.com

References

[1] ITU-T Recommendation H.265 and ISO/IEC 23008-2, ITU-T and ISO/IEC JTC 1. High Efficient Video Coding (HEVC). 2013. Available from: http://handle.itu.int/11.1002/1000/11885

[2] Sullivan GJ, Ohm J, Han WJ, Wiegand T. Overview of the high efficiency video coding (HEVC) standard. IEEE Transactions on Circuits and Systems for Video Technology. 2012;**22**(12):1649-1668

[3] Bahri N, Belhadj N, Grandpierre T, Ben Ayed MA, Masmoudi N, Akil M. Real-time H264/AVC encoder based on enhanced frame level parallelism for smart multicore DSP camera. Journal of Real-Time Image Processing. 2016; **12**(4):791-812

[4] Ohm J, Sullivan GJ, Schwarz H, Tan TK, Wiegand T. Comparison of the coding efficiency of video coding standards-including high efficiency video coding (HEVC). IEEE Transactions on Circuits and Systems for Video Technology. 2012;**22**(12): 1669-1684

[5] Kim J, Jun DS, Jeong S, Cho S, Choi JS, Kim J, et al. An SAD-based selective Bi-prediction method for fast motion estimation in high efficiency video CodingC. ETRI Journal. 2012;**34**(5): 753-758

[6] Yoo HM, Suh SJW. Fast coding unit decision algorithm based on inter and intra prediction unit termination for HEVC. In: IEEE International Conference on Consumer Electronics (ICCE). 2013. pp. 300-301

[7] Choi K, Park SH, Jang ES. Coding tree pruning based CU early termination, document JCTVC-F092. Joint Collaborative Team on Video Coding. 2011. Available from: https://www.itu.int/wftp3/av-arch/jctvc-site/2011_07_F_Torino/

[8] Yang J, Kim J, Won K, Lee H, Jeon B. Early SKIP detection for HEVC, document JCTVC-G543. Joint Collaborative Team on Video Coding. 2011. Available from: https://www.itu.int/wftp3/av-arch/jctvc-site/2011_07_F_Torino/

[9] Bossen F, Flynn D, Sharman K, Suhring K. Joint collaborative team on video coding (JCT-VC) of ITU-T SG16 WP3 and ISO/IEC JTC1/SC29/WG11. HM Software Manual; 2014. Available from: https://usermanual.wiki/Pdf/softwaremanual.2114962307/help

[10] Software reference test model HM16.2. 2016. Available from: https://hevc.hhi.fraunhofer.de/

[11] Khemiri R, Kibeya H, Loukil H, Sayadi FE, Atri M, Masmoudi N. Real-time motion estimation diamond search algorithm for the new high efficiency video coding on FPGA. Analog Integrated Circuits and Signal Processing. 2018;**94**(2):259-276. DOI: https://doi.org/10.1007/s10470-017-1072-6

[12] Rehman S, Young R, Chatwin C, Birch P. An FPGA based generic framework for high speed sum of absolute difference implementation. European Journal of Scientific Research. 2009;**33**(1):6-29

[13] Nalluri P, Alves LN, Navarro A. A novel SAD architecture for variable block size motion estimation in HEVC video coding. In: IEEE International Symposium on System on Chip (SoC). 2013. pp. 1-4

[14] Nalluri P, Alves LN, Navarro A. High speed SAD architectures for variable block size motion estimation in HEVC video coding. In: IEEE International Conference on Image Processing (ICIP). 2014. pp. 1233-1237

[15] Khemiri R, Kibeya H, Sayadi FE, Bahri N, Atri M, Masmoudi N. Optimisation of HEVC motion estimation exploiting SAD and SSD GPU-based implementation. IET Image Processing. 2018;**12**(2):243-253

[16] Nalluri P, Alves LN, Navarro A. Improvements to TZ search motion estimation algorithm for multiview video coding. In: International Conference on Systems, Signals and Image Processing (IWSSIP); Austria. 2015. pp. 388-301

[17] Kibeya H, Belghith F, Ben Ayed MA, Masmoudi N. Fast coding unit selection and motion estimation algorithm based on early detection of zero block quantified transform coefficients for high-efficiency video coding standard. IET Image Processing. 2016;**10**(5): 371-380

[18] Belghith F, Kibeya H, Loukil H, Ben Ayed MA, Masmoudi N. A new fast motion estimation algorithm using fast mode decision for high-efficiency video coding standard. Journal of Real-Time Image Processing. 2014;**11**(4):675-691

[19] Liquan S, Zhi L, Xinpeng Z, Wenqiang Z, Zhaoyang Z. An effective CU size decision method for HEVC encoders. IEEE Transactions on Multimedia. 2013;**15**(2):465-470

[20] Qin Y, Xinfeng Z, Siwei M. Early termination of coding unit splitting for HEVC. In: IEEE Signal and Information Processing Association Annual Summit and Conference (APSIPA ASC); Asia-Pacific. 2012

[21] Podder PK, Paul M, Murshed M. Fast mode decision in the HEVC video coding standard by exploiting region with dominated motion and saliency features. PLoS One. 2016;**11**(3):1-12. Available from: https://doi.org/10.1371/journal.pone.0150673

[22] Khemiri R, Bahri N, Belghith F, Sayedi FE, Atri M, Masmoudi N. Fast motion estimation for HEVC video coding. In: IEEEIPAS'16: International Image Processing Applications and Systems Conference. 2016. pp. 1-4

[23] Gweon RH, Lee JL, Lim J. Early termination of CU encoding to reduce complexity HEVC. JCTVC-F045. 2011. Available from: https://www.itu.int/wftp3/av-arch/jctvc-site/2011_07_F_Torino/

[24] Liu H, Jie Y. Fast HEVC intra mode decision based on hybrid cost ranking. Advances in Multimedia. 2016;**3**:1-9. London: Hindawi Publishing Corporation; DOI: http://dx.doi.org/10.1155/2016/5164025

[25] Frank B, Benjamin B, Karsten S, David F. HEVC complexity and implementation analysis. IEEE Transactions on Circuits and Systems for Video Technology. 2012;**22**((12): 1685-1696

[26] Dıaz-Honrubia A, Martinez J, Cuenca P. HEVC: A Review, Trends and Challenges. Second Workshop on Multimedia Data Coding and Transmission. 2011

[27] Nalluri P, Alves LN, Navarro A. Fast motion estimation algorithm for HEVC. In: IEEE Second International Conference on Consumer Electronics. 2012

[28] ISO/IEC. ITU-T Joint Exploration Test Model (JEM) Reference Software. 2017. Available from: https://jvet.hhi.fraunhofer.de/

[29] García-Lucas D, Cebrián-Márquez G, Díaz-Honrubia AJ, Cuenca P. Acceleration of the integer motion estimation in JEM through pre-analysis techniques. Journal of Supercomputing. March 2019;**75**(3):1203-1214. DOI: 10.1007/s11227-018-2352-3

Chapter 3

Digital Image Processing Applied to Optical Measurements

Alonso Saldaña-Heredia, Pedro Antonio Márquez-Aguilar, Álvaro Zamudio Lara and Arturo Molina-Ocampo

Abstract

Digital image processing is a useful tool that improves pictorial information for human interpretation and is mainly used for storage, transmission, and representation of different data. In this chapter, we want to introduce an optical technique which couples physical analysis with image processing for a measurement system. Optical methods were used to obtain the stress-strain relation by different invasive and noninvasive methods. This chapter talks about a novel noninvasive methodology to measure stress-strain evolution; this technique is based upon a single laser beam reflected on the cross section of ductile materials (steel and aluminum) while they are under a compression load. The way we measure one laser beam is by using the Gaussian beam propagation equations; we propose that the reflection area of the laser is going to change as the material surface area is compressed and we analyze these differences by using digital image processing. With this technique we are able to construct a stress-strain diagram.

Keywords: compression test, stress-strain, Gaussian beam, Fourier analysis, image processing

1. Introduction

In this chapter, we introduce a new methodology to measure the stress-train relation for ductile materials subjected to a continuum axial load; this loading was carried out by means of a universal testing machine. To obtain the stress-strain relation, materials were submitted to standardized compression tests, and to develop the technique, we used a laser beam impacting the cross section of the materials; the laser reflection was studied through Gaussian beam propagation equations and digital image processing. The scope of the present research is to determine a relation between the free propagation of a Gaussian beam and the stress-strain evolution of a ductile material.

Stress-strain diagrams are very important in understanding the behavior of materials under different loads [1]; these diagrams show the elastic, plastic, and rupture characteristics of materials. There are two methods to obtain these diagrams.

First, the invasive methods from which mechanics draw by doing physical tests, such as the test tube in which a standardized probe is placed on a testing machine; a continuum load is applied to it, and the resulting deformation is measured [2]. Other invasive methods are optical methods, which can determine residual stress, in-field displacements, and strain. Here, hole drilling is the most used technique.

Originally developed in 1930 by Mathar [3], it is nowadays a standardized technique by the ASTM [4].

Second, nondestructive or noninvasive optical methods such as multiple laser displacement sensors which are applied to piping systems [5], stress measurements using crystal curvature technique during film growths [6], and another technique called deflectometry [7, 8], in which light passes through arrays that measure the curvature of objects; they are proposed as mirrors. The reflection caused by these objects is seen in a CCD camera, and the pattern is studied with standard phase shift techniques; most of the used objects are aspherical.

An image was defined as a two-dimensional function: $f(x,y)$ where x and y are plane coordinates and the amplitude f at any pair of coordinates (x,y) is called the intensity referred as a gray level of the image at that point [9]. One of the first applications of digital images was in the newspaper industry through the introduction of the Bartlane cable picture transmission system in the early 1920s, where specialized printing equipment coded pictures for cable transmission and then reconstructed them at the receiving end [9]. However, the image processing method itself required storage and computational power; nevertheless, by this time, it was not possible to talk about processing since the development of the computer hadn't arrived. One of the first works in this field was done by Harry Andrews [10], whom introduced techniques in order to work with images as matrixes; another book about the treatment of pictures was introduced by 1976 [11].

Digital image processing has been applied widely, in such cases as in control level for industries [12], which is based on the treatment of a special light shape generated by a laser, also measuring displacements in infrastructures by a matrix of points [13]. Some researchers around the application in engineering are evaluating the curvature of a pipeline using a parabolic function to determine its deformation [14], analyzing the location of cracks in reinforced concrete by monitoring the surface deformation with two cameras [15], strain measurements during film stretching process following the digital changes of the marker [16], and measuring the strain in time for standardized fatigue tests [17], among others.

In this chapter we introduce a novel methodology to measure the stress-strain behavior of ductile materials; this technique uses a laser beam focused on the cross section of a material probe which is under a compression test. We propose that the materials (1018 steel and aluminum alloy) will act as optical spherical mirrors. This is due to their surface transformation; the laser focuses in a surface which is completely flat, and it will deform as a reaction of the compression test. Therefore, the laser strikes this surface, and acting as a "mirror," it will reflect and scatter the beam. Thus, the reflected laser area will increase as the deformation increases. This laser reflection is analyzed with Gaussian beam propagation equations by using digital image processing to measure each increasing area. This is the procedure we follow to obtain a relation between the laser-beam-free propagation and the strain, which we propose to be similar to the cross-section deformation of both materials. We show the accuracy, error, and sensitivity of the methodology, and we theoretically demonstrate how the laser beam spreads; the present research can be a suitable technique as it only uses a single laser beam for stress-strain characterization.

2. Theory

2.1 Gaussian beam analysis

The Gaussian beam is the simplest, the most known, and the most worked with, because its characteristics and evolution are well-known [18]. The amplitude function represented from Gaussian beams can be deduced by applying boundary conditions in the optical resonator, where the laser radiation is produced; this amplitude is described by

$$E(x,z) = E_0 \frac{\omega_0}{\omega(z)} \cdot exp\left[\frac{-x^2}{[\omega(z)]^2} - \frac{kx^2}{2R(z)} - kz + \eta(z)\right], \tag{1}$$

where E_0 is the electric field amplitude, ω_0 is the beam waist, $\omega(z)$ is how the beam propagates, k is the wave number ($k = 2\pi/\lambda$), λ is the wavelength, $R(z)$ is the curvature radius of the spherical waves, and $\eta(z)$ is the beam phase angle [19]. Laser beams are able to pass through different media; the light reflection occurs when it arrives to the boundary separating two media of different optical densities, and some of the energy is reflected back into the first medium [20]; taking this outset, if a laser beam strikes a mirror, the reflection can be studied as a Gaussian propagation. In our case, the metallic surface will be modeled as a convex mirror. As it is well-known, there is a relation between the focal length and the curvature radius of a mirror. Using this relation the phase of the transmitted wave is altered to

$$\varphi(x,z) = 2\eta(z) - \frac{kx^2}{z\left(1+\frac{{z_0}^2}{z^2}\right)} + \frac{kx^2}{f}, \tag{2}$$

where z_0 is the initial Rayleigh distance and f is the focal length of the mirror [21]. To study the propagation through a lens phenomenon, the Gaussian propagation equations are established in which ω_0 and z_0 turns into ω_1 and z_1, respectively, after a distance f and they are calculated by

$$\omega_1 = \frac{\omega_0}{\sqrt{\left(1+\frac{{z_0}^2}{f^2}\right)}}, \tag{3}$$

$$z_1 = \frac{f}{\left(1+\frac{f^2}{{z_0}^2}\right)}. \tag{4}$$

This pair of equations involves how Gaussian beam propagates [21], so in order to calculate the new beam waist in the propagation axis, we have

$$\omega(z_p) = \omega_1\sqrt{\left(1+\frac{{z_p}^2}{{z_1}^2}\right)}, \tag{5}$$

where $\omega(z_p)$ is the new beam waist at z_p which is the propagation distance.

The goal of this research is to reach a general relation between the strains caused in any material by measuring with one laser beam, its reflection and relating it to a focal length transformation. As we implicate the focal length, we need these Gaussian propagation equations to calculate the changes in the focal length during the compression test. Substituting Eqs. (3), (4) in (5) it can be deduced:

$$\frac{{z_p}^2}{{z_0}^4} \cdot x^2 + x\left(1 - \frac{\omega(z_p)^2}{{\omega_0}^2}\right) - {z_0}^2 = 0. \tag{6}$$

The parameter z_p is calculated doing DIP, taking each area increment per second during the compression test. Once the result from Eq. (6) is obtained, the variation of the focal length is determined applying

$$\xi = \frac{f_f - f_i}{f_i}, \tag{7}$$

where f_f is the final focal length and f_i is the initial focal length; following this procedure, we obtained a dimensionless variable.

2.2 Compression tests

Mechanical tests are used to know the mechanical properties of materials; a compression test enables the user to understand the behavior of a material under a continuum axial load; from this test it is possible to obtain the stress-strain diagram of any material [2]. In this chapter we worked with samples of steel with dimensions of $2.5 \times 2.5 \times 2.2$ cm and aluminum samples of $1 \times 1 \times 0.9$ cm according to the small-type standard dimensions [22]; all samples undergo into compression test according to ASTM E-9 [22]. The tests were performed with a speed ratio of 0.2 cm/s up to 90 MPa for steel and up to 20 MPa for aluminum. Since we are working on the elastic part of the diagram, therefore we can apply Hooke's law:

$$\sigma = E \cdot \varepsilon, \tag{8}$$

where σ is the engineering stress, E is the Young's module of the material (200 and 70 GPa) for steel and aluminum, respectively, and ε is the engineering strain. We propose that the experimental stress is going to behave similar to the Hooke's law; thus, we relate Eq. (8) to the focal length by

$$\sigma = E \cdot K \cdot \xi, \tag{9}$$

where K is a material coefficient proposed in this chapter and ξ is the dimensionless value obtained in Eq. (7). The coefficient K is obtained from the relation between the slopes of both graphs of interest: stress-strain diagram and DIP plot.

2.3 Theoretical analysis

In this research, we used a He-Ne laser with specific parameters such as initial intensity, beam waist, and Rayleigh distance that are shown in its handbook [23].

In **Figure 1** we plot Eqs. (1) and (2) substituting the results from Eq. (7), the initial parameters of our laser and propagating formally this laser beam. In this figure, we can observe that when the focal length increases, the beam waist has also an increase, in this theoretical demonstration; we propose that these increments are proportional as we assume that $\varepsilon \approx f$.

By using Fresnel diffraction and the treatment of lens transmission [24], we have

$$U_f(u,v) = \frac{exp^{\left[\frac{ik}{2f}\left(u^2+v^2\right)\right]}}{i\lambda f} * \iint_{-\infty}^{\infty} U(x,y) \cdot t_A \cdot exp^{\left[\frac{ik}{2f}(xu+yv)\right]} \mathrm{dxdy}, \tag{10}$$

where

$$t_A = exp^{\left[\frac{ik}{2f}\left(x^2+y^2\right)\right]} \tag{11}$$

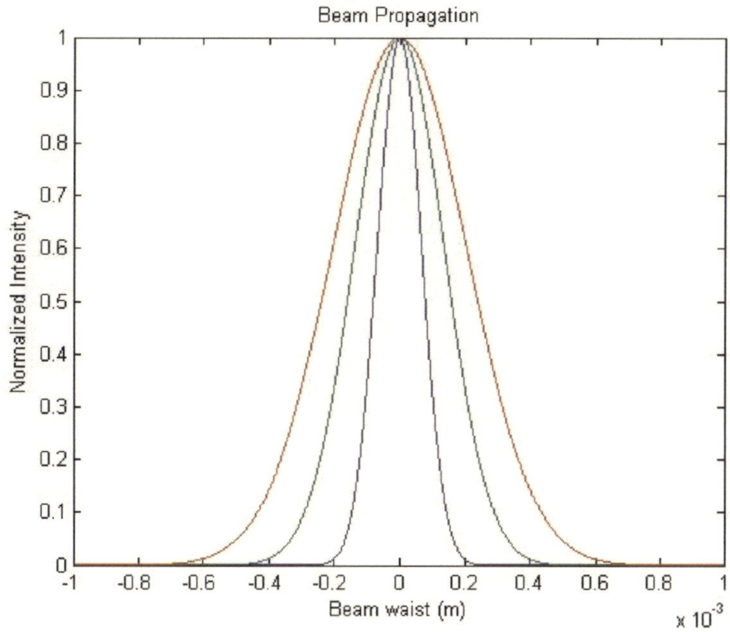

Figure 1.
Gaussian propagation: intensity profile.

and

$$U(x,y) = exp^{-[(x^2+y^2)]}. \tag{12}$$

Replacing Eqs. (11) and (12) into Eq. (10), expanding formally and changing coordinates, we obtain

$$U(\rho) = \frac{i\pi}{a\lambda f} exp^{\left[\left(\frac{ik}{2f}+\frac{b^2}{4a}\right)\cdot\rho^2\right]}, \tag{13}$$

where

$$a = \left(1 - \frac{ik}{2f}\right), \tag{14}$$

$$b = \frac{ik}{f}, \tag{15}$$

According to the present research, the initial area of the reflected laser was $A \sim 0.009\ m^2$.

3. Methodology

As we established before, we use two ductile materials: steel and aluminum; in total, seven samples were hand-sanded and polished in the same manner to mirror grade in the laser-impact section, and they were placed in the machine perpendicular to the piston to begin the compression test. A diagram of this method is shown schematically in **Figure 2a**. The output of a He-Ne laser (L), with a wavelength

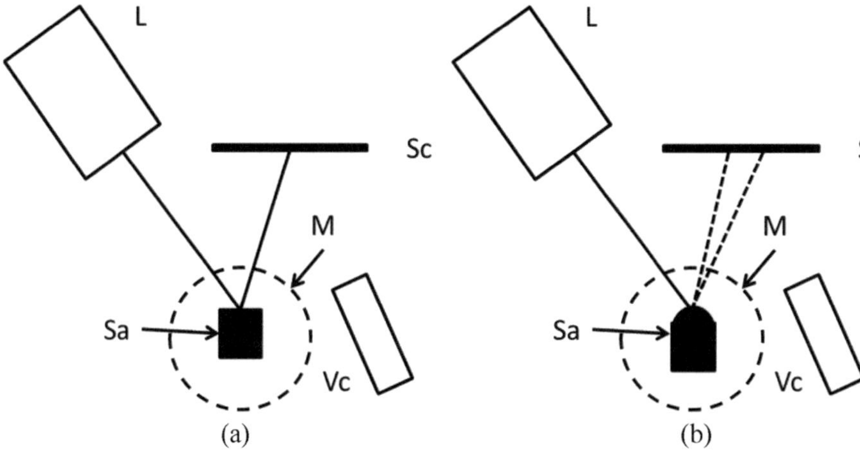

Figure 2.
Experimental setup: (a) material with no strain; (b) the strained material will scatter light.

λ = 632 nm and a power of 1 mW, is placed 15 cm from the sample (Sa) in order to irradiate the polished face, and then, the reflected beam impacts a screen (Sc) which is placed 10 cm beside the laser beam and parallel to the sample. The material is first completely flat, with no stress, and as it is compressed with the universal machine (M), the size of the cross section will decrease as a reaction (**Figure 2b**). During the tests, the deformation rate was 0.2 cm/s with duration of 5 min approximately, and while they were taking place, the reflected light was recorded with a video camera (Vc) which is placed in front and parallel to the screen aside the sample. All tests were done at room temperature, and samples were compressed around 2 mm.

When we finish the mechanical test, a post-processing is carried out:

1. First, we need to transfer the video from the video card to the computer.

2. Then, we use the free software called *Video to JPG converter*; it helps us to divide the entire video into each frame. The software enabled us to turn our videos with an average of 54 frames per second.

3. A program is written in Matlab® for digital image processing.

To do the image processing, we used some Matlab® toolbox functions, mention, and describe them:

- *imread*: this function loads the image as a matrix.

- *rgb2grey*: this code turns the colored image into a gray scale level.

- *im2bw*: this is necessary to convert the image matrix into a binary code.

- *bwarea*: we call this function at the end of the code to calculate by binary code the total area of the reflected laser beam.

Along **Figure 3**, we can observe how the code works: in **Figure 3a** it is seen how *imread* works; when we call it, the image is loaded; for **Figure 3b** we can observe how *rgb2grey* converts the colored image into a grayscale; in **Figure 3c** we called

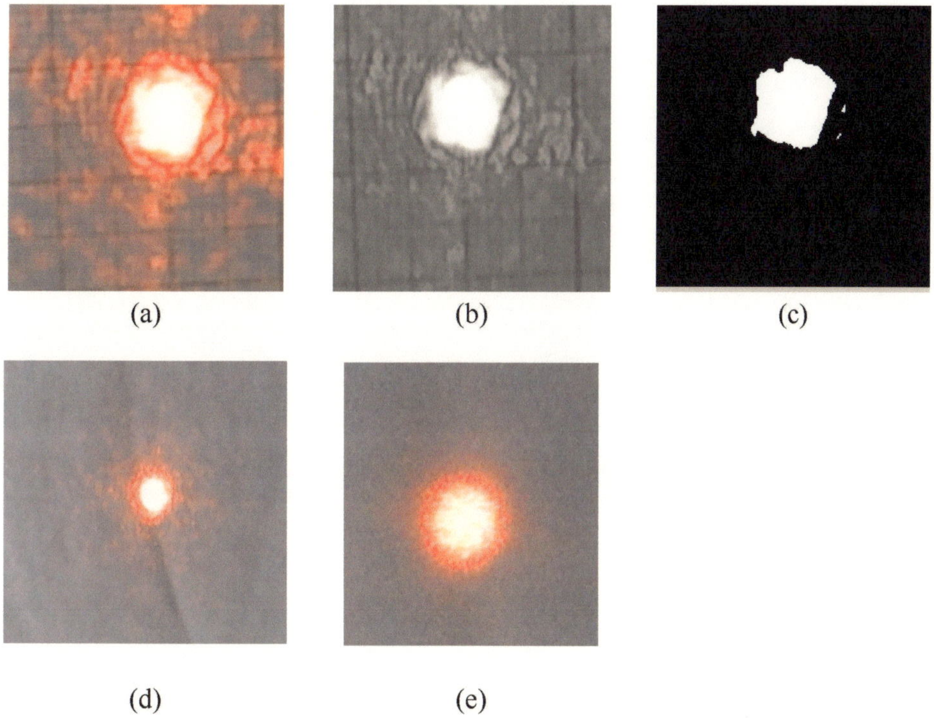

Figure 3.
Image processing: (a) how the image is loaded; (b) grayscale image; (c) binary image; (d) initial beam diameter; (e) beam diameter at $t = t_i + \Delta t$.

im2bw to do a binary code of the image. At this step we can apply the function *bwarea* to know the area of this "circle." We can observe in **Figure 3d** and **e** how the beam diameter increases, for a $t_i = 0$ s and $t_f = \Delta$t s. By following the methodology described and using Eq. (6), we can obtain the change in the focal length and relate it to the deformation in the material.

The code was written to repeat this process iteratively for every image. We propose that the calculated area is the parameter $\omega(z_p)$. Therefore Eq. (6) is used to calculate the focal length. We know that as a result of doing a mechanical test, we can obtain a stress-strain diagram; it is calculated through strain gages and special software incorporated to the machine. At the end of the iterative process, we plot the focal length differences following Eq. (7).

4. Results

Along this chapter, we have mentioned that we prepared four steel samples and three aluminum probes, to test them under standardized compression test; for each one we obtained two graphs of interest, the stress-strain diagram and the DIP plot; **Figure 4** shows these two graphs of interest. **Figures 4–8** correspond to steel samples.

In **Figure 4a** we show the stress-strain diagram obtained from the software of the machine; in **Figure 4b** we can observe the related stress-focal length diagram obtained by following the experimental procedure and using Eq. (9). In the graphs we can observe a linear behavior. In section 2.2, we propose an equation related to Hooke's law, where the K value is calculated using the slopes of each graph and $\Delta\varepsilon$ is taken from 0.1 to 0.3%ε. Therefore the calculated slope of the real stress-strain

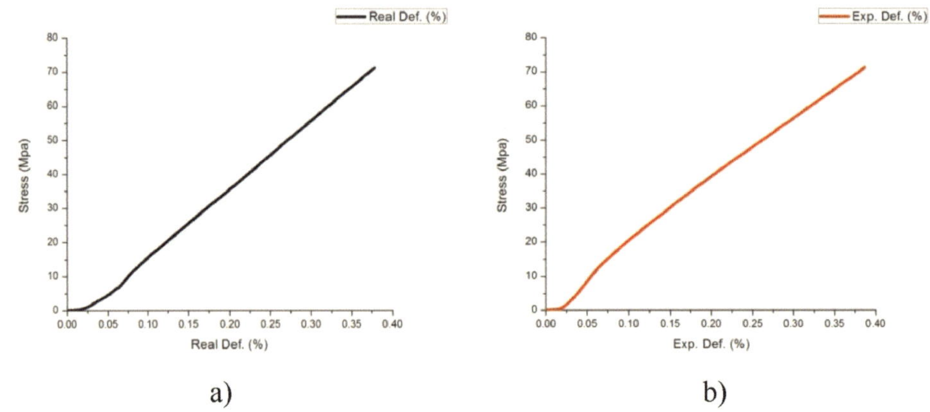

Figure 4.
Stress-strain diagrams: (a) obtained from universal machine, (b) experimentally from optical treatment.

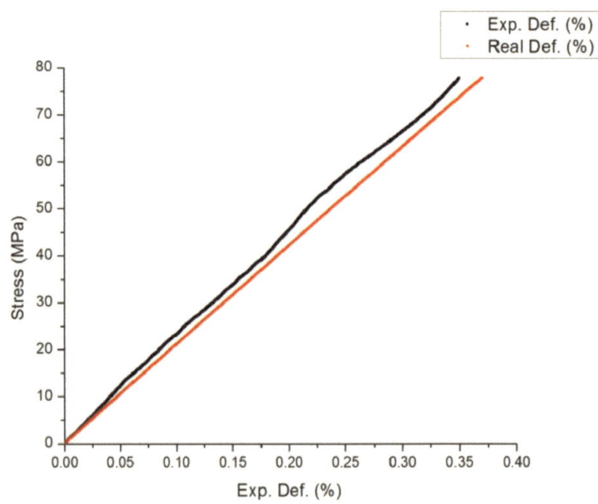

Figure 5.
Comparison between stress-strain diagrams for steel's sample 1.

diagram is 0.00351 and for the experimental data is 0.001401; *K* coefficient between them is 2.5.

In **Figure 5** we show the first steel sample comparison between the real strain (Real Def.) and the experimental related-strain (Exp. Def.); both are represented in % as strain has no dimensions, and also some statistical results are shown in **Table 1**. From here, the following graphs are going to be presented the same way.

We repeat this procedure for the next three samples, obtaining *K* factor and comparing the real stress-strain diagram with the experimental plot and showing the statistical results for each one.

For the second test, we can see in **Table 2** that *K* factor remains in a value of 2.5; in this test we obtained an accurate result of 88% as compared to the real graph. In the third and fourth tests, we see in **Tables 3** and **4** that the value of the proposed *K* factor decreases to 2.4, but we obtained the same approach in reproducing the stress-strain diagram.

In **Figures 5** and 7, the behavior of the experimental graph is above the real stress-strain diagram; for **Figures 6** and **8**, the behavior has an intersection—it first starts below then crosses above it. We propose that the behavior of the area increase

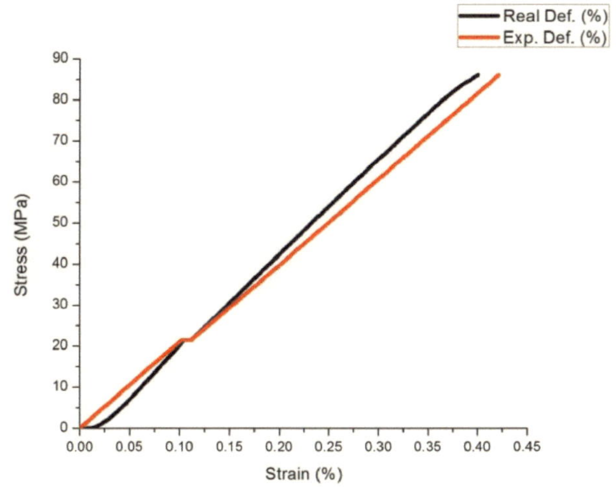

Figure 6.
Comparison between stress-strain diagrams for steel's sample 2.

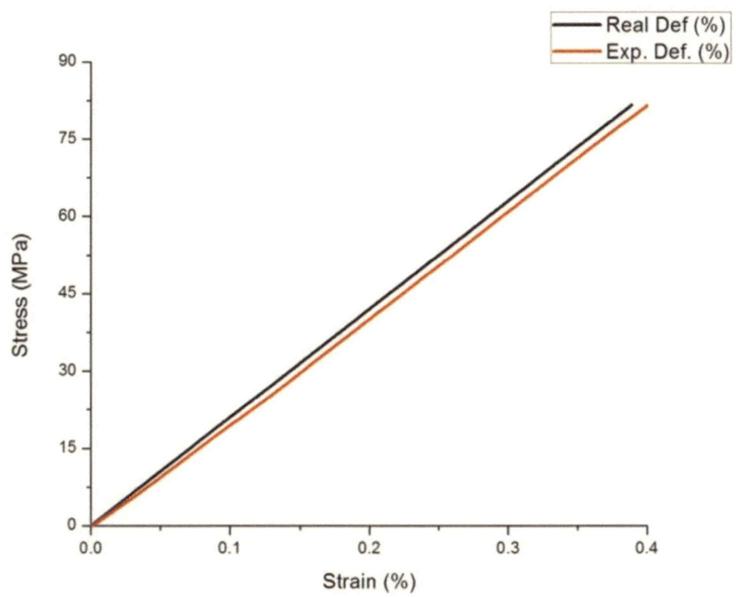

Figure 7.
Comparison between stress-strain diagrams for steel's sample 3.

is due to the material surface, as it was hand-sanded and polished; light is not reflecting equally in every sample of material.

In **Table 5** we summarize the accuracy and mean error for this four strain measurements; we can observe that the mean accuracy of our methodology is 89%.

With this novel technique, taking the focal length as a parameter for measuring the stress-strain relation of a material, we proved an 89% effectiveness following standardized compression tests using steel samples; also we obtained a K value for this material of 2.5, which establishes the relation between the slopes of the real and the experimental graphs [25].

In this section, we present the statistical results and stress-strain diagrams obtained from aluminum samples. We are following the same process by comparing the DIP graph with the real stress-strain obtained from the universal machine

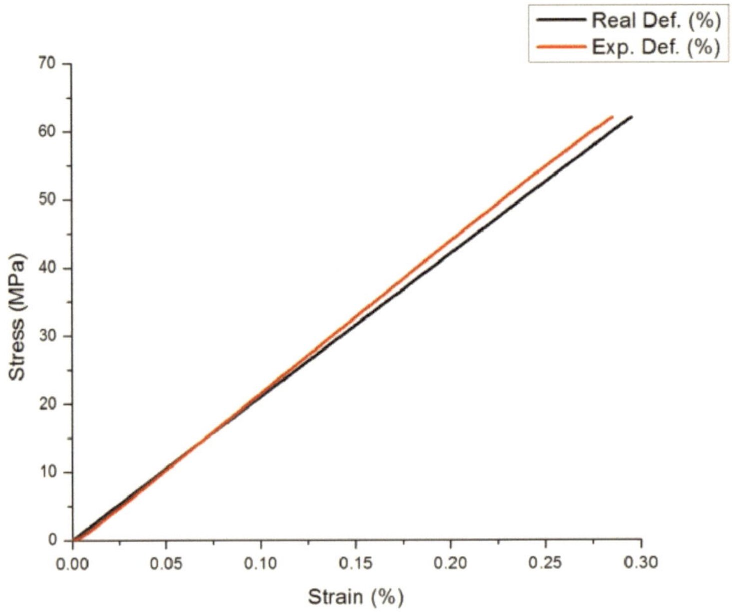

Figure 8.
Comparison between stress-strain diagrams for steel's sample 4.

First sample	
K factor	2.5
Young's modulus E	188 ± 12 GPa
% difference from 200 GPa	11%
Standard deviation	0.011

Table 1.
Statistical result for steel's sample 1 during the compression tests and Gaussian beam analysis.

Second sample	
K factor	2.5
Young's modulus E	188 ± 12 GPa
% difference from 200 GPa	11%
Standard deviation	0.010

Table 2.
Statistical results for steel's sample 2 during the compression tests and Gaussian beam analysis.

Third sample	
K factor	2.4
Young's modulus *E*	188 ± 12 GPa
% difference from 200 GPa	11%
Standard deviation	0.012

Table 3.
Statistical results for steel's sample 3 during the compression tests and Gaussian beam analysis.

Fourth sample	
K factor	2.4
Young's modulus *E*	187 ± 13 GPa
% difference from 200 GPa	11%
Standard deviation	0.013

Table 4.
Statistical results for sample 4 during the compression tests and Gaussian beam analysis.

Sample	Accuracy (%)	*K*
1	89	2.5
2	89	2.5
3	89	2.4
4	89	2.4

Table 5.
Accuracy and error of the four tests.

software. **Figure 9** and **Table 6** show the results for the first aluminum sample; with this material we obtained a *K* value of 4.52 and an approach of 90%.

Using aluminum samples, we obtained similar approximations to the steel ones. In **Table 7** we can observe a *K* value of 4.54 and a slightly less approach than sample 1, obtaining 89%. In **Table 8** we observe a *K* value of 4.5 and an approach of 88%.

By comparing **Figures 9–11** to steel results, we can see that aluminum alloys behave differently than steel ones. In these figures we can appreciate that the experimental graph goes above the real diagram at the same point (0.08%). In **Figures 10** and **11**, the experimental result goes first below, then above the real stress-strain diagram. These differences, such as steel ones, are due to the sample surface; during the process of making mirror-grade samples, we can accidentally cause nonuniform surfaces, and thus light reflection is not always the same.

In **Table 9** we summarize the accuracy and mean error for these three measurements; it is seen that the mean accuracy of our method is 89%.

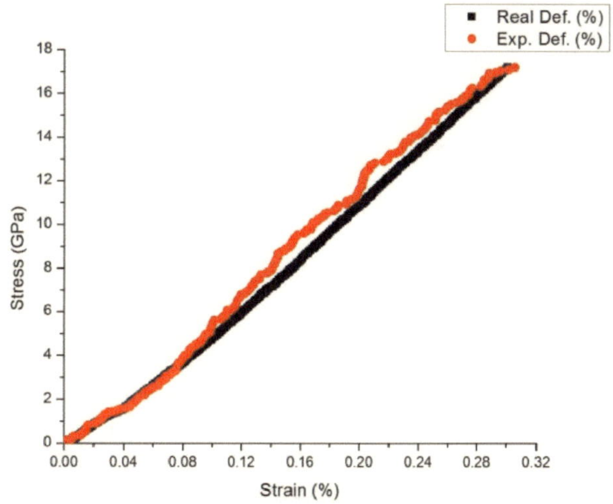

Figure 9.
Comparison between stress-strain diagrams for aluminum's sample 1.

First sample	
K factor	4.52
Young's modulus *E*	63 ± 7 GPa
% difference from 70 GPa	10%
Standard deviation	0.015

Table 6.
Statistical results for aluminum's sample 1 during the compression tests and Gaussian beam analysis.

Second sample	
K factor	4.54
Young's modulus *E*	62 ± 8 GPa
% difference from 70 GPa	11%
Standard deviation	0.013

Table 7.
Statistical results for aluminum's sample 2 during the compression tests and Gaussian beam analysis.

Third sample	
K factor	4.5
Young's modulus *E*	61 ± 9 GPa
% difference from 70 GPa	12%
Standard deviation	0.018

Table 8.
Statistical results for aluminum's sample 3 during the compression tests and Gaussian beam analysis.

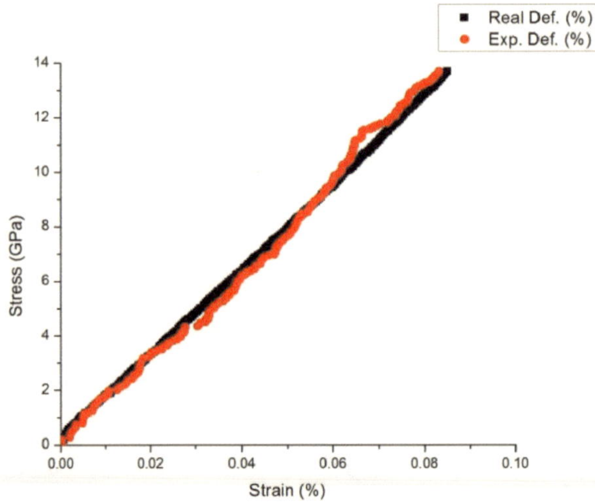

Figure 10.
Comparison between stress-strain diagrams for aluminum's sample 2.

With this developed technique, taking the focal length as a parameter for measuring the stress-strain relation of a material, we proved an 89% effectiveness following standardized compression tests using aluminum samples; we also obtained a *K* value for this material of 4.5, which stablishes the relation between the slopes of the real and the experimental graphs [26].

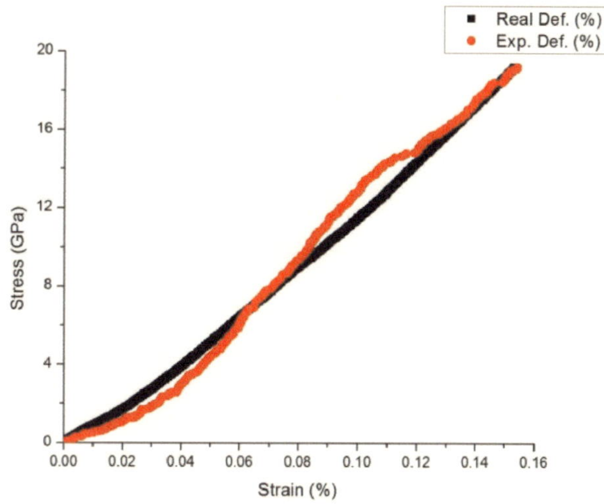

Figure 11.
Comparison between stress-strain diagrams for aluminum's sample 3.

Probe	Accuracy (%)	*K*
1	90	4.54
2	89	4.52
3	88	4.5

Table 9.
Accuracy and error of the three tests.

Summarizing these tests, steel and aluminum, we observed that the present methodology can measure the stress-strain relation of a ductile material with an average error of 11%. We established that by recording the video, we obtained 54 images in average; therefore, we calculate the mean differences between measurement in a 10-s time interval, thus to obtain the sensitivity of this methodology, which resulted to 27 microdeformations.

5. Conclusion

The stress-strain relation of two ductile materials under standardized compression test was measured using one laser beam, its reflection, and digital image processing treatment; we obtained 89% of accuracy and a relation of 27 microdeformation. Also it was demonstrated that the diameter of the laser reflection has an increment according to the increase in the focal length; we also showed following Fresnel diffraction and the transmission through a lens that the comparison between the reflected area and the experimental results is congruent.

Acknowledgements

Alonso Saldaña Heredia wants to thank CONACYT for the grant no. 360140.

Conflict of interest

The authors declare no conflict of interest for this chapter.

Author details

Alonso Saldaña-Heredia[1]*, Pedro Antonio Márquez-Aguilar[2], Álvaro Zamudio Lara[2] and Arturo Molina-Ocampo[2]

1 Metropolitan Polytechnic University of Hidalgo—UPMH, Tolcayuca, Mexico

2 Research Center on Engineering and Applied Sciences—IICBA, Autonomous University of Morelos State, Cuernavaca, Mexico

*Address all correspondence to: aheredia@upmh.edu.mx

References

[1] Figliola R, Beasley F. Theory and Design for Mechanical Measurements. 5th ed. USA: John Wiley & Sons; 2011. 605 p. ISBN: 978-0-470-54741-0

[2] Gere J, Goodno B. Mecánica de Materiales. 8th ed. Cengage Learning: Mexico; 2016. 1125 p. ISBN: 978-1-111-57773-5

[3] Mathar J. Determination of initial stresses by measuring the deformation around drilled holes. Transactions of the ASME. 1934;**56**(4):249-254

[4] ASTM. Determining residual stresses by the hole-drilling strain gage method. In: ASTM Standard Test Method E837-08. West Conshohocken, PA: American Society for Testing and Materials; 2008

[5] Maekawa A et al. Development of noncontact measurement methods using multiple laser displacement sensors for bending and torsional vibration stresses in piping systems. International Journal of Pressure Vessels and Piping. 2015;**137**:38-45. DOI: 10.1016/j.ijpvp.2015.05.002

[6] Premper J et al. In situ stress measurements during pulsed laser deposition of $BaTiO_3$ and $SrTiO_3$ atomic layers on Pt(0 0 1). Applied Surface Science. 2015;**335**:44-49

[7] Liu Y et al. Fast and accurate deflectometry with crossed fringes. Advanced Optical Technologies. 2014;**3**(4):441-445

[8] Huang E et al. Measuring aspheric surfaces with reflection deflectometry. SPIE Newsroom. 2013. 3 p. DOI: 10.1117/2.1201309.005087. Available from: https://www.researchgate.net/publication/275085156_Measuring_aspheric_surfaces_with_reflection_deflectometry/link/554d1c9f0cf21ed2135f5dca/download

[9] González R, Woods R. Digital Image Processing. 2nd ed. New Jersey: Prentice Hall; 2002. 793 p. ISBN: 978-0-201-18075-6

[10] Andrews HC. Computer Techniques in Image Processing. NY: Academic Press; 1970

[11] Rosenfeld A, Kak CA. Digital Picture Processing. NY: Academic Press; 1982

[12] Li C et al. Digital image processing technology applied in level measurement and control system. Procedia Engineering. 2011;**24**:226-231

[13] Kim S-W, Kim N-S. Multi-point displacement response measurement of civil infrastructures using digital image processing. Procedia Engineering. 2011;**14**:195-203

[14] Iwamoto T, Kanie S. Evaluation of bending behavior of flexible pipe using digital image processing. Procedia Engineering. 2017;**171**:1272-1278

[15] Rimkus A et al. Processing digital images for crack localization in reinforced concrete members. Procedia Engineering. 2015;**122**:239-243

[16] Muniandy K et al. Online strain measurement during blown film extrusion using digital image correlation. Journal of Mechanical Engineering. 2018;**5**:154-165

[17] Blug A et al. Real-time GPU-based digital image correlation sensor for marker-free strain-controlled fatigue testing. Applied Sciences. 2019;**9**:1-15

[18] Alda J. Laser and Gaussian beam propagation and transformation. Encyclopedia of optical Engineering.

2003. 16 p. Available from: https://www.researchgate.net/publication/255041663_Laser_and_Gaussian_Beam_Propagation_and_Transformation/link/00463522b465e900a9000000/download

[19] Yariv A. Quantum Electronics. 3rd ed. U.S.A.: John Wiley & Sons; 1990. 693 p. ISBN: 978-0-471-60997-1

[20] Wood R. Physical Optics. 3rd ed. Washington DC: Optical Society of America; 1988. 846 p. ISBN: 155-752-0631

[21] Saleh AEB, Teich MC. Fundamentals of Photonics. 1st ed. New York: John Wiley & Sons; 1991. 982 p. ISBN: 978-0-585-32147-9

[22] ASTM E-9, ICS Number Code 77.040.10 (Mechanical testing of metals). DOI: 10.1520/E0009-09

[23] JDSU Self-Contained Helium-Neon Laser Systems 1500 series Specification Sheet. JDS Uniphase Corporation 10138846 005 0512 SCHNL1500.DS.CL.AE. 2012

[24] Goodman JW. Introduction to Fourier Optics. 3rd ed. United States: Roberts & Company; 2005. 509 p. ISBN: 0-9747077-2-4

[25] Saldaña HA, Márquez APA, Molina OA. Laser-beam reflection for steel stress-strain characterization. Measurement. 2018;**113**:92-98

[26] Saldaña HA, Márquez APA, Molina OA. Aluminum strain measurement by beam propagation. In: Martínez-García A et al., editors. Emerging Challenges for Experimental Mechanics in Energy and Environmental Applications. Proceedings of the 5th International Symposium on Experimental Mechanics and 9th Symposium on Optics in Industry (ISEM-SOI), Conference Proceedings of the Society for Experimental Mechanics Series. 2015. DOI: 10.1007/978-3-319-28513-9_2

Chapter 4

Experimental and Theoretical Investigation on the Shear Behaviour of High Strength Reinforced Concrete Beams Using Digital Image Correlation

Touhami Tahenni and Thibaut Lecompte

Abstract

In this chapter an experimental investigation is carried out on high strength concrete beams without transverse reinforcement and with transverse reinforcement. The beams were tested in bending under two concentrated loads using the technique of digital image correlation. In the test setup, the shear zone which is defined by the area of beam between the support point and the loading point was studied by the camera of high resolution. The Gom-Aramis software was used to record and analyse the numerical images by determination of the deformation of concrete in the compressed zone of the beam, to calculate the opening, the spacing and the length of the diagonal cracks. The experimental shear strength of the beams was compared with the theoretical values predicted by the different design codes, such as the American ACI 318, the British Standard BS 8110, the European Eurocode 2, the New Zealand NZS 3101 and the Indian Standard IS456. The results show that all the design codes underestimate the contribution of high strength concrete to the shear resistance of reinforced concrete beams, and greatly overestimate the contribution of transverse reinforcement. The European Eurocode 2 is the only one among the four code models that gives the best prediction of the ultimate shear strength of high strength concrete.

Keywords: beam, high strength concrete, shear capacity, cracking, digital image correlation

1. Introduction

The shear behaviour of high strength concrete (HSC) beams is an interest research despite the abundance of literature on the subject. However, the principal of this solicitation remains insufficiently explained because up to now, there are no analytical methods which give in detail the different factors influencing shear capacity of HSC beams. For this reason, a number of empirical models, based on testing reinforced concrete beams, are used by the different design codes throughout the world to determine the shear strength of reinforced concrete beams, particularly in the seismic zone. Moreover, the HSC is considered as a new building

 IntechOpen

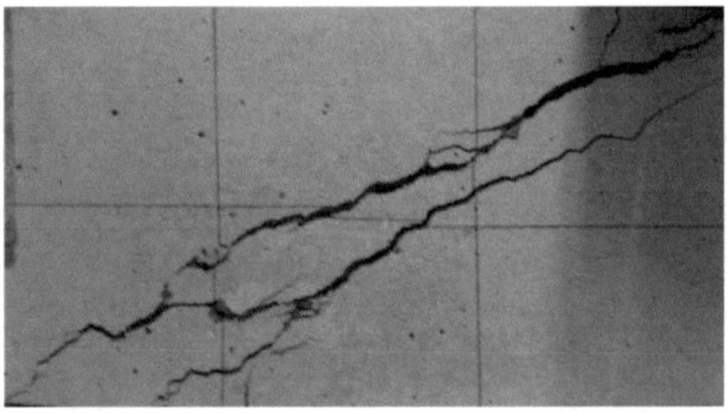

Figure 1.
Diagonal cracking crossing the aggregates in HSC.

material, and there is a lack of base data for shear strength of HSC beams, so all the models proposed by the design codes and developed essentially for normal strength concrete (NSC) were extrapolated to HSC, to validate the applicability of these empirical methods to this material. More investigation work is then required to cover this aspect and provide further information.

The present chapter aims to improve the structural behaviour of HSC beams particularly the shear, and thus ameliorate the performance of the built environment to ensure an adequate durability of constructions.

The HSC presents a low resistance under shear [1–3] because the crack surfaces are smooth and cross the aggregates particles as shown in **Figure 1**, which shows a low contribution of the aggregates in the shear strength. However, the HSC is characterised by high compressive strength and by better adhesion with steel reinforcement, which gives a best contributions of the compression zone and the dowel action effect to the shear strength of HSC beams.

2. Experimental program

2.1 Materials used and concrete mix design

There is no single branded procedure available for mix proportion for HSC, therefore careful selection of the materials is also effective in production of HSC [4]. The ACI 318 [5] defines HSC as concrete with a compressive strength >41 MPa.

The concrete used to prepare the HSC beams is made from the following constituents:

Cement: cement used in this work was an Ordinary Portland Cement of type CEM I 52.5 N CE CP2 NF, and was provided by Lafarge group (cement of St-Pierre-la-Cour of Laval in France). The density of this cement is 3160 kg/m^3 and its specific surface is 3520 cm^2/g, therefore falling within the range of cements that can formulate a HSC (between 3500 and 4000 cm^2/g) [6]. The particle sizes vary between 0 and 100 μm.

Fine aggregate: the sand used to make a HSC must have a modulus of fineness greater than or equal to 2.8. The Sand with a modulus of fineness <2.5 makes the concrete sticky and therefore difficult to compact and less resistant [7]. Rolled sand from the Loire region in France, is used for the present work, with a granular class of 0/4 (mm). The fineness modulus of this sand was measured at a value between 2.9 and 3.1. This sand also has a water demand of <0.5% of its mass.

Coarse aggregate: to make the HSC, the ideal granulate must be crushed, cleaned, of regular shape, with a reduced angularity, and containing less flat particles or elongated [8, 9]. Crushed gravel from quartz, with a granular class of 4/15 (mm) is used for the present work. This gravel has a water demand of the order of 2–3% of its mass.

Fine mineral additions: fine mineral additions consisting of blast furnace slag and limestone fillers. The slag additives were finely ground to give a specific surface of 7000 cm^2/g and were used in proportion of 10% by weight of cement. This type of addition was provided by Ecocem in France. The fine limestone fillers is Betocarb®HP-EB, manufactured by the Omya-Meac Group in France, and were used in proportion of 23% by weight of cement. The mineral additives were used to fill in the finer gaps between the aggregates and hence to improve the density and the compactness of the concrete material.

Superplasticizer: a high range water reducing admixture (HRWRA) in a liquid form, based on polycarboxylates (CHRYSO Fluid Optima 206), was used in a proportion of 2.5% by weight of cement. It is interesting to add the superplasticizer in 1/3 of the quantity with the mixing water to ensure the dispersion of the cement grains, and 2/3 remaining at the end of mixing [10].

Water: potable tap water is used.

The mix designs used in making the HSC beams are presented in **Table 1**.

2.2 Mechanical properties of concrete

The compressive strengths of HSC used in making the beams without transverse reinforcement and with transverse reinforcement were measured through the crushing tests of cylindrical concrete specimens of 80 mm diameter by 160 mm in height, using a press with capacity of 500 kN. Measurements of the longitudinal compressive strains were carried out with the help of an extensometer (**Figure 2**) and enabled the modulus of elasticity of the HSC. The results were recorded in a data acquisition system (**Figure 3**) for the complete stress-strain curve of HSC (**Figure 4**).

The tensile strength was also evaluated for the HSC by splitting tests of concrete cylinders, 80 mm in diameter and 160 mm in height.

Figure 4 shows that the pre-peak behaviour is quasi-linear with greater rigidity, and the average ultimate deformation (ε_{cu} = 2%) decreases with the increase in the compressive strength, which is below the ultimate deformation required by the different universal design codes (ε_{cu} = 3.5%) which reflects a decrease in ductility. It should be noted that the HSC specimens exhibit brittle and explosive fracture resulting from a lack of ductility, major disadvantage of this material, as shown in **Figure 2**.

The results of the compressive strength f_c, the tensile strength f_t and the modulus of elasticity E_c of HSC are shown in **Table 2**.

2.3 Steel reinforcement

The longitudinal reinforcement composed of two high yield bars of 10 mm diameters in the top zone of the beam (compression), two high yield bars of 8 mm diameters in the bottom zone of the beam (tension) and 6 mm for the transverse reinforcement in the form of stirrups, as shown in **Figures 6(a)** and 7. The steel was

Cement	Slag (10%)*	Limestone filler (23%)*	Gravel	Sand	Water	Admixture (2.5%)*	W/C	Slump test (cm)
382.5	38.25	88.0	1029	700	148.8	9.56	0.38	15

**By weight of cement.*

Table 1.
Mixing ingredients of HSC (kg/m³).

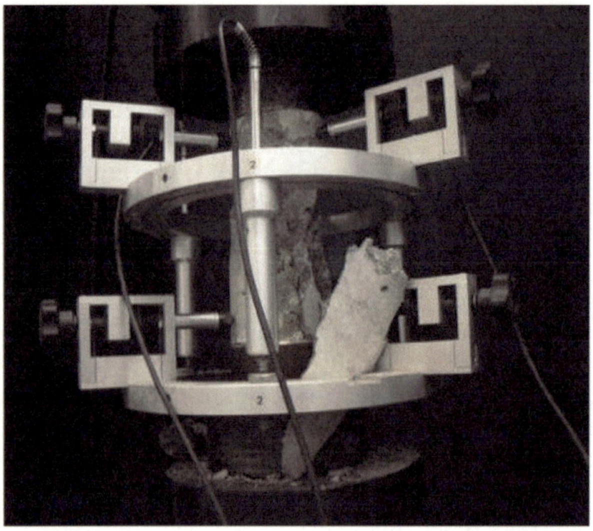

Figure 2.
Concrete cylinder compression test.

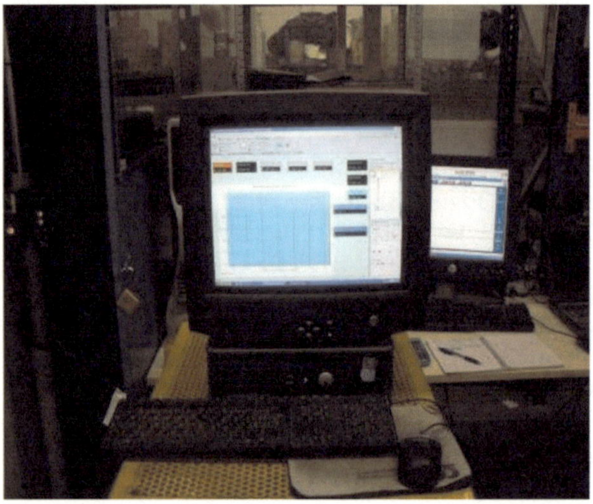

Figure 3.
Data acquisition system for the compression test.

tested under direct tension using a machine with capacity of 500 kN to determine the Young's modulus and the elastic limit. Measurement of the current deformations is carried out by Gom-Aramis software [11] using Digital Image Correlation (DIC) technique (**Figure 5**). The test results give a Young's modulus of 204 GPa and an elastic limit of 500 MPa.

2.4 Beam specimens and testing procedure

A total of six reinforced HSC beams divided into two series were cast:

- The first series of beams without transverse reinforcement, noted 'Series A'.
- The second series of beams containing transverse reinforcement in the form of stirrups, noted 'Series B'.

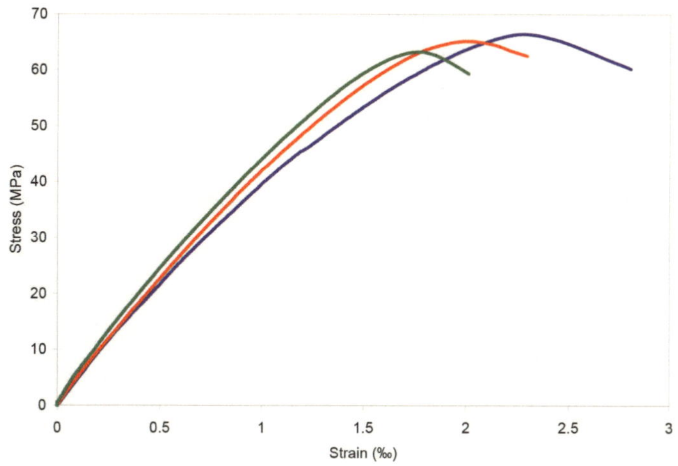

Figure 4.
Stress-strain curve in compression of HSC.

f_c (MPa)	E_c (GPa)	f_t (MPa)
65 (±3)	45.2 (±5)	6 (±1)

Table 2.
Average mechanical properties of HSC.

To find a precision in the experimental results, three beams were tested in each series.

The beams were tested under monotonic static loading using a 250 kN servo-controlled hydraulic jack (**Figure 8**). The details of the beams tested are presented in **Table 3**. It is noted that the value of shear-span/effective depth ratio (a/d) is within the a/d ranges leading to a dominant shear behaviour which results in a shear failure of the reinforced concrete beams [6, 12–16].

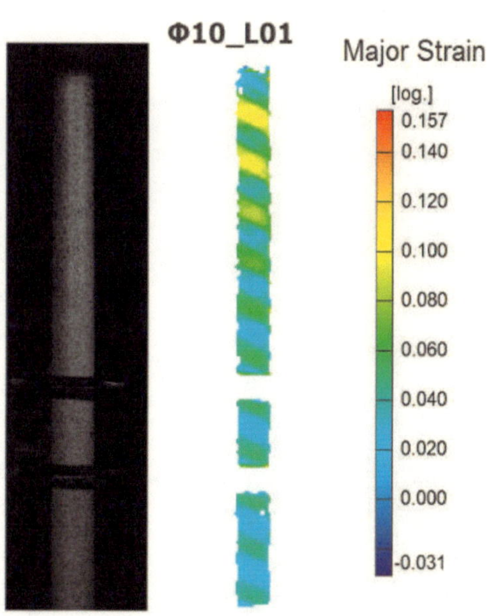

Figure 5.
Direct tensile test and measurement of the steel deformations by Gom-Aramis software (using DIC).

Figures 6 and 7 illustrate the casting of the beams and the detail of reinforcement. A highly sensitive video camera was used to detect the development of cracks, monitor the evolution of the diagonal cracks as the load was gradually increased and measure their widths (**Figure 8**). The analysis of the DIC is

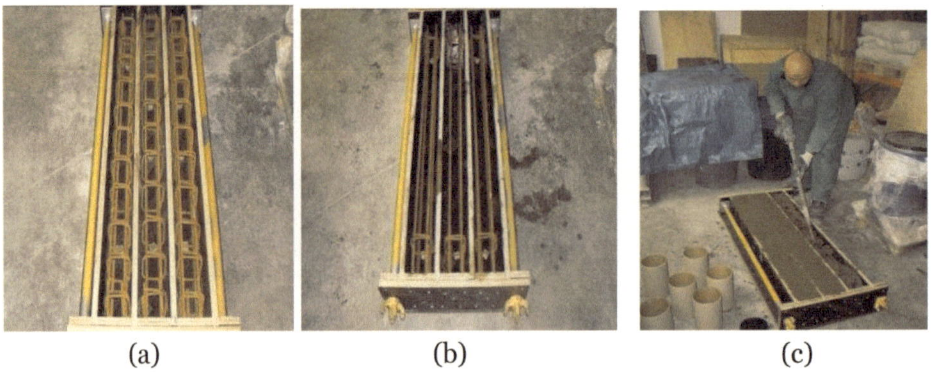

Figure 6.
Formwork and manufacture of beams. (a) Beams with stirrups, (b) beams without stirrups, and (c) casting of beams.

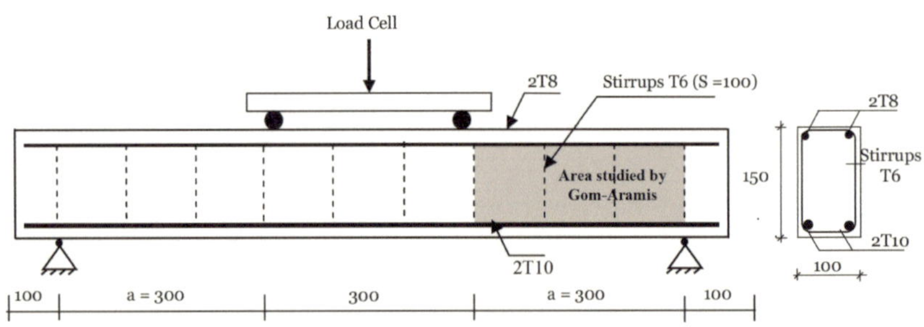

Figure 7.
Reinforcement of the beam and the flexural devise.

Figure 8.
Four-point bending test with the camera.

Identification of beams	b (mm)	h (mm)	d (mm)	a/d	ρ_s (%)	ρ_w (%)	f_y (MPa)
Series A	100	150	135	2.2	1.16	0.00	500
Series B	100	150	129	2.3	1.16	0.56	500

b = width of beam; h = height of beam; a/d = shear-span/effective depth; ρ_s = longitudinal reinforcement ratio; ρ_w = transverse reinforcement ratio; f_y = yield strength of longitudinal reinforcement.

Table 3.
Details of the tested beams.

Figure 9.
Image analysis by Gom-Aramis software.

performed by Gom-Aramis software [11] (**Figure 9**) to obtain the deformation of concrete and to monitor the crack evolution in terms of width, spacing and length.

3. Analysis of results

3.1 Development of cracks and failure modes of the beams

The vertical flexural cracks are the first type developed in the bottom zone of beam between the two point landings; this is the tension zone. The effect of stirrups is considered negligible before the formation of the diagonal cracking. From a loading rang of 60–70% of total ultimate load, the diagonal crackling is occurred from the flexural cracks (**Figure 11(b)**) within the shear zone between the support of the beam and the loading point (**Figure 10(b)**). In the Series A of the beams, the diagonal cracking formed independently of flexural cracks. When this cracking presents a sufficiently width, the failure was also by diagonal cracking as shown in **Figure 10(a)**. This mode of failure is designated by shear.

The addition of the transverse reinforcement in the Series B of the beams retards the appearance of the diagonal cracking and limits their opening and therefore prevents the shear failure of the beam and changes the failure mode of the beam, from shear to flexure. When the diagonal cracking is sufficiently penetrated in the compression zone between the two loading points, the concrete is crushed as shown in **Figure 10(b)**. This mode of failure is designated by shear-compression. This series of beams showed no cracking along the longitudinal reinforcements and have developed many diagonal cracks. Generally, the diagonal cracking is inclined of about 45° with the longitudinal axis of the beam as shown in **Figures 10(a)** and **11(d)**.

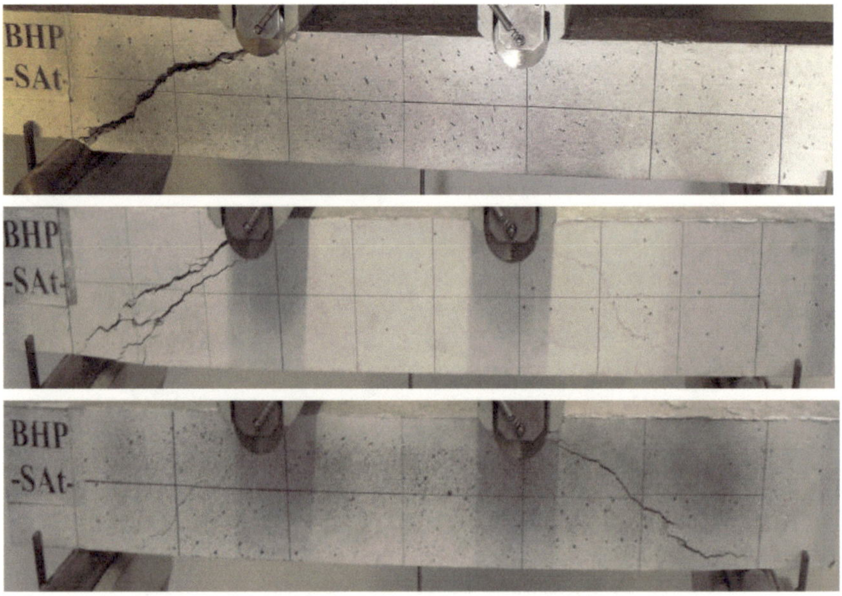

(a)

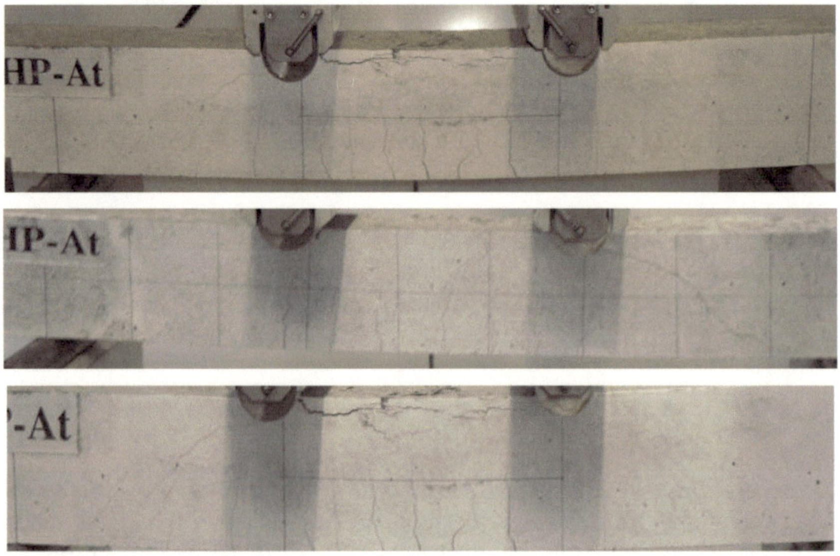

(b)

Figure 10.
Cracks and failure patterns of beams. (a) Failure of Series A (HSC beams without transverse reinforcement) and (b) failure of Series B (HSC beams with transverse reinforcement).

Table 4 gives the average experimental results of the first crack loads (P_{cr}), the diagonal cracking loads (P_d) and the total ultimate loads (P_u) for all tested beams. The presence of the transverse reinforcements improves the resistance reserve of the beams beyond the diagonal cracking. An increase in the ultimate load varies of around 50% has been recorded for the Series B by comparison to Series A. Comparable results have been reported in the literature [12–15] on reinforced concrete beams made of different strength of concrete ranging from 20 to 68 MPa. This shows that the effect of the transverse reinforcement is practically the same in any type of concrete.

A typical monitoring of a diagonal cracking using DIC is shown in **Figure 11**.

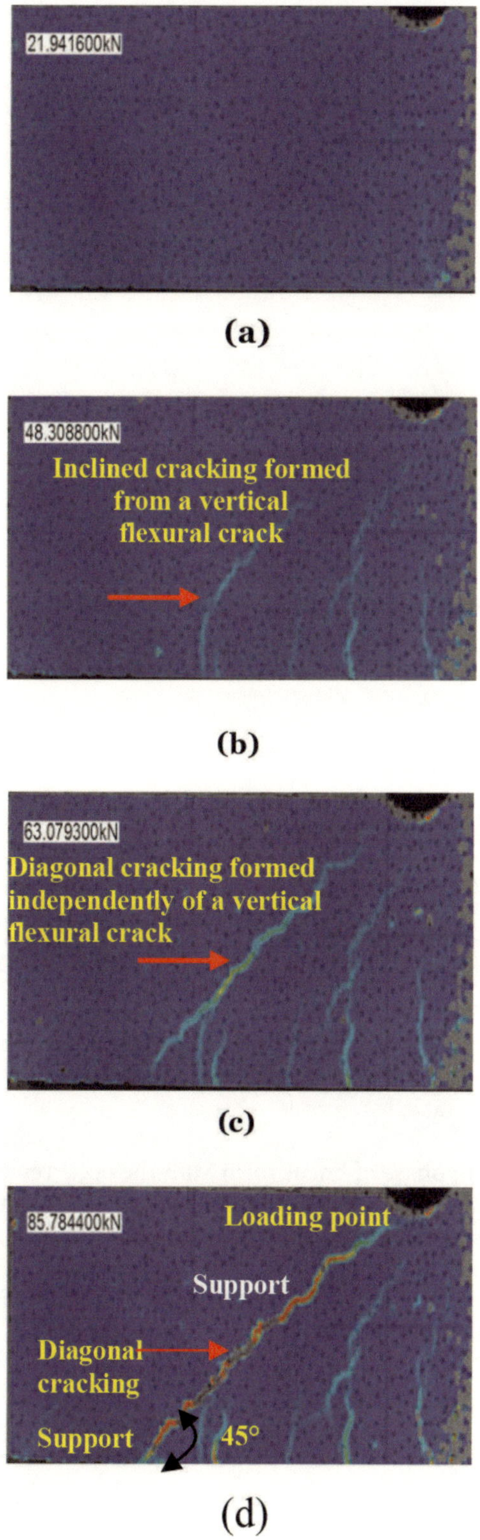

Figure 11.
A sequence of crack development within a shear zone in Series B (photos obtained by digitizing video Gom-Aramis). (a) At 24% of ultimate load—no cracking in the shear zone. (b) At 60% of ultimate load—inclined cracking (width = 0.01 mm). (c) At 70% of ultimate load—diagonal cracking (width = 0.04 mm). (d) Just prior to failure—diagonal cracking (width = 0.16 mm).

Identification of beams	P_f (kN)	P_d (kN)	P_u (kN)	Mode of failure
Series A	16.50	43.79	60.00	Shear
Series B	18.75	60.62	86.18	Flexion shear-compression

Table 4.
Diagonal cracking load and ultimate load of the tested beams.

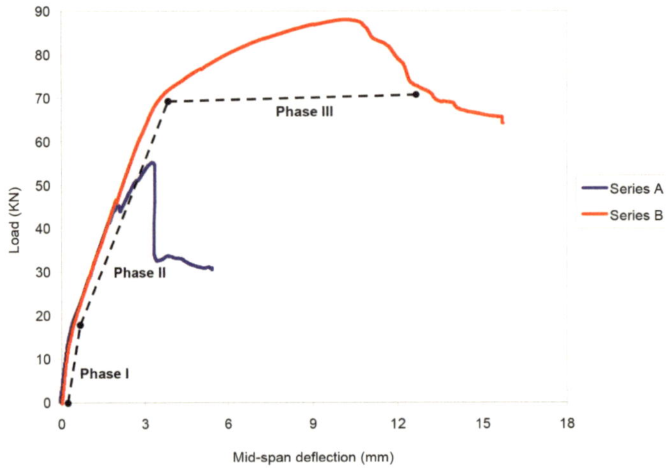

Figure 12.
Load-deflection curves for the HSC beams.

3.2 Load-deflection characteristics

One LVDT was attached to the bottom surface of the beams at mid-span to measure the deflection. From the load-deflection curves (**Figure 12**), it can be seen that the behaviour of the beams with transverse reinforcement (Series B) shows three main phases:

- **Phase I:** presents a linear form where the deflection increases at the same time as the load; this is the elastic behaviour of the beams up to the appearance of the first flexural crack.
- **Phase II:** a second phase of linear form after the occurrence of the first flexural crack. The deflection increases with the load but with relatively higher values. In this phase, the cracks are sufficiently developed in length and opening, the Series A of the beams (without transverse reinforcement) lose their rigidity and fail without undergoing further sufficient deflection (**Figure 13**) compared to those containing transverse reinforcement (Series B).
- **Phase III:** corresponds to the plastic behaviour of the beams, where the deflection is not proportional to the load with higher deformation of concrete before the failure of the beams. This phase illustrates the ductile behaviour as shown in **Figure 14**.

3.3 Shear analysis of HSC beams

3.3.1 Theoretical analyses of the shear force

The ultimate shear force V_u in 'kN' of reinforced concrete beam is determined by the contribution of the compression zone V_{cy}, the contribution of the aggregate

Figure 13.
Brittle shear failure (Series A).

Figure 14.
Ductile behaviour (Series B).

interlocking V_{ay}, the contribution of the longitudinal reinforcement V_d and the contribution of the stirrups V_s as shown in Eq. (1) and **Figure 15**. This can be written as:

$$V_u = V_{cy} + V_{ay} + V_d + V_s \tag{1}$$

$(V_{cy} + V_{ay} + V_d)$ expresses the shear resistance of concrete V_c, and the Eq. (1) is simplified as follows:

$$V_u = V_c + V_s \tag{2}$$

The three shear forces which present the contribution of the concrete to shear strength are evaluated by Taylor [17] and by Paulay and Fenwick [18] as follows:

- V_{cy} = 20–40% of V_u
- V_{ay} = 35–50% of V_u
- V_d = 15–25% of V_u

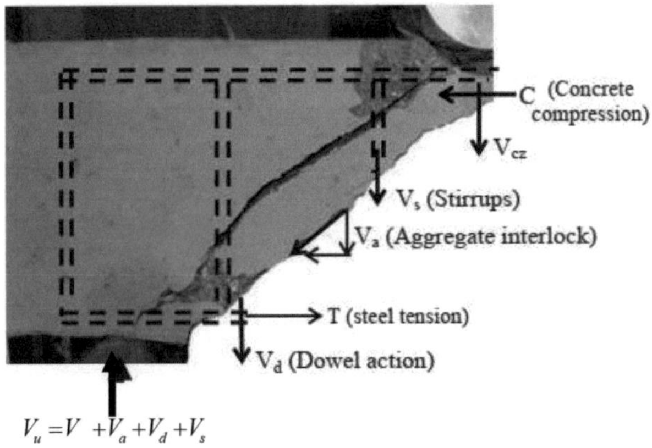

Figure 15.
Mechanism of shear forces in a beam with transverse reinforcement [15].

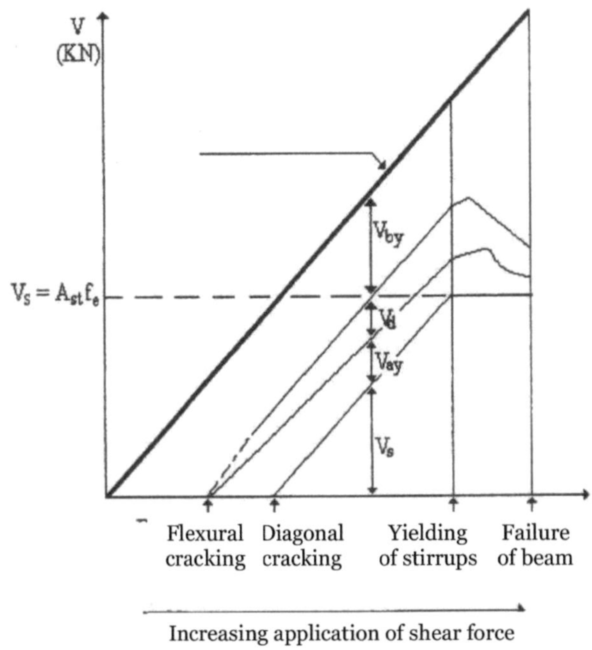

Figure 16.
Distribution of shear force in a reinforced concrete beams [17].

Figure 16 shows the contribution of the different components of ultimate shear force (V_u) in a reinforced concrete beams as shown in **Figure 14** and given by Eq. (1).

Table 5 presents the theoretical models to determine the ultimate shear strength of reinforced concrete beams, given by the different universal design codes.

3.3.2 Comparison between test results and theoretical predictions of the shear strength

Figure 17 shows the experimental and the theoretical ultimate shear forces predicted by the five universal design codes presented in **Table 5** above, for two series of beams. The Series A is not transversely reinforced ($V_s = 0$) so the ultimate shear force of this series represents the contribution of concrete to the shear resistance (V_c). As shown in this figure, the five models underestimate the contribution

DOI: http://dx.doi.org/10.5772/intechopen.86499

Codes	Model of the total ultimate shear force V_u (kN)	Explanation
ACI 318 [5]	$V_u = \frac{1}{7}\left(\sqrt{f_c} + 120\rho\frac{d}{a}\right) b_w d + \frac{A_v f_{sv} d}{s}$	f_c = cylinder compressive strength f_{ck} = characteristic compressive strength = $f_c/0.8$ d = effective depth of beam a = shear span b_w = width of beam A_v = section of stirrup f_{sv} = yield strength of stirrups s = stirrups spacing $\rho = A_s/b_w d$ A_s = section of longitudinal reinforcement f_{cu} = cube compressive strength γ_m = material partial safety factor for shear, taken as 1.25 α = inclination of stirrups (α = 90°) θ = angle between inclined concrete struts and the main tension chord (θ = 45°) $k = 1 + \sqrt{\frac{200}{d}}$, d (mm) z = lever arm = $0.9d$
BS 8110 [19]	$V_u = \frac{0.79}{\gamma_m}(100\rho)^{\frac{1}{3}}\left(\frac{400}{d}\right)^{\frac{1}{4}}\left(\frac{f_{cu}}{25}\right)^{\frac{1}{3}} b_w d + 0.87\frac{A_v f_{sv} d}{s}$ for $a/d \geq 2$ $V_u = \left(2\frac{d}{a}\right)\frac{0.79}{\gamma_m}(100\rho)^{\frac{1}{3}}\left(\frac{400}{d}\right)^{\frac{1}{4}}\left(\frac{f_{cu}}{25}\right)^{\frac{1}{3}} b_w d + 0.87\frac{A_v f_{sv} d}{s}$ for $a/d < 2$	
Eurocode 2 [20]	$V_u = 0.18\left[k.(100.\rho f_c)^{\frac{1}{3}}\right] b_w d + \frac{A_v f_{sv} z(\cot\theta + \cot\alpha)}{s}\sin\alpha$	
NZS 3101 [21]	$V_u = (0.07 + 10\rho)\sqrt{f_c} b_w d + \frac{A_v f_{sv} d}{s}$	
Indian Standard IS456 [22]	$V_u = \frac{0.85\sqrt{0.8 f_{ck}}\left(\sqrt{1+5\beta}-1\right)}{6\beta} b_w d + \frac{A_v f_{sv} d}{s}$ where $\beta = \frac{0.8 f_{ck}}{6.89(100\rho)} > 1$	

Table 5.
Theoretical models of the ultimate shear strength given by different codes.

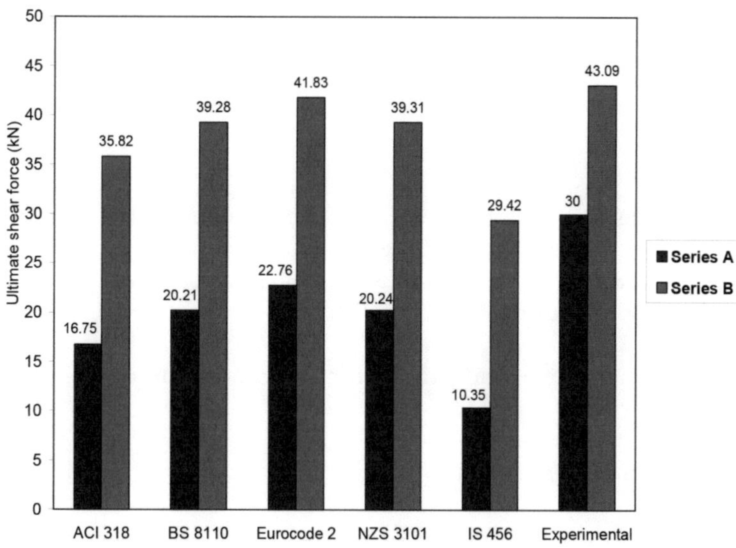

Figure 17.
Experimental and predicted values of the shear strength of HSC beams.

of HSC material to the shear strength of reinforced concrete beams. An average around 40% of underestimating was recorded. Among the five models, The European Eurocode 2 gives the best predictions with underestimating of around 24% the shear strength of HSC beams. By comparison, the Indian Standard IS456 is the most conservative to predict the ultimate shear force of HSC beams with a prediction of around 65% below the experimental results. This requires more effort and research to extrapolate and to valid these models developed essentially for normal strength concrete to HSC and therefore faithfully reflect the contribution of this new material to the shear strength of reinforced concrete beams.

The Series B of the beams is transversely reinforced by stirrups, the ultimate shear force of this series represents the contribution of concrete (V_c) and the contribution of stirrups (V_s) to the shear strength of HSC beams. The ultimate shear strength of this series is also shown in **Figure 17**. The concrete contribution V_c represents 70% of the total shear force and the steel contribution V_s represents 30%. Therefore, the presence of the transverse reinforcement has improved the ultimate shear strength of HSC beams by around 30%. The five design codes greatly overestimate the contribution of the stirrups to the shear strength of HSC beams. An average overestimation is around 45% was recorded. This is due to the fact that the contribution of the stirrups to the shear strength developed in the five code models is based on the yielding of this reinforcement; this is the Ritter [23] and Mörsch [24] truss analogy. The analogy proposes that a reinforced concrete beam failing after yielding of the transverse reinforcement, and before the crushing of concrete. In all tested beams, the failure mode is characterized by crushing of concrete after the complete penetration of the diagonal cracking in the compression zone of the beam as shown in **Figure 10(b)**, and in the same time the transverse reinforcements have not yielding. The contradiction between the analogy of Ritter and Mörsch and the experimental observations led to a greatly overestimation of the transverse reinforcement contribution to the shear strength of reinforced concrete beams.

On adding up the contribution of concrete and the contribution of the stirrups to the shear strength of HSC beams, Eurocode 2 seems to give the best predictions for the ultimate shear strength compared to other code models.

The five universal design codes require more refinement to reflect the real contributions of both materials; the HSC and the steel reinforcement, to the shear resistance of high strength reinforced concrete beams.

4. Conclusion

A Series of high strength reinforced concrete beams under shear was investigated. The effects of the concrete and the transverse reinforcement on the shear behaviour of the beams were verified. The experimental and the theoretical results led to the following conclusion:

- The HSC is sudden, expressing the brittleness and the low ductility of this material.

- The Series A of beams, without stirrups exhibit a relatively fragile behaviour.

- The addition of the stirrups in the Series B of the HSC beams, improves the ductility of this series. The improvement of the ductility is particularly needed in the regions of higher seismicity to avoid the catastrophic failure of structures.

- The diagonal cracking is efficiently restrained by the stirrups, because their occurrence is delayed and their opening is very fine and did not exceeds the serviceability limit of crack width (W_k = 0.3 mm).

- The digital image correlation technique gives best and very precise results.

- The ultimate shear resistance of HSC beams is increased with the presences of the stirrups. An increase of around 50% was recorded.

- The contribution of the HSC to the shear resistance of reinforced concrete beams was underestimated by the five universal design codes, and in the same time, the contribution of the stirrups was overestimated. These design codes need more refinement to reflect and to ascertain the improved shear strength of high strength reinforced concrete beams.

Acknowledgements

The experimental investigation presented in this chapter was sponsored by the Ministry of Higher Education and Scientific Research of Algeria. The tests were carried out at Laboratory of Engineering of the Materials of Bretagne (LIMATB) at the University of Bretagne Sud, Lorient, France. Also, Dr. Thibaut Lecompte is gratefully thanked for their willing discussion and active participation in the project.

Author details

Touhami Tahenni[1*] and Thibaut Lecompte[2]

1 Department of Technology, Faculty of Sciences and Technology, Djilali Bounaama University of Khemis Miliana, Khemis Miliana, Algeria

2 Université de Bretagne-Sud, Lorient, France

*Address all correspondence to: touhami_tahenni@yahoo.fr

References

[1] Pendyala RS, Mendis P. Experimental study on shear strength of high strength concrete beams. ACI Structural Journal. 2000;**97**(4):564-571

[2] Johnson MK, Ramirez JA. Minimum shear reinforcement in beams with higher strength concrete. ACI Structural Journal. 1989;**86**(4):376-382

[3] Cladera A, Mari AR. Experimental study on high-strength concrete beams failing in shear. Engineering Structures. 2005;**27**:1519-1527

[4] Khuntia M, Stojadinovic B. Shear strength of reinforced concrete beams without transverses reinforcement. ACI Structural Journal. 2001;**98**(5):648-656

[5] ACI Committee 318. Building Code Requirements for Structural Concrete: (ACI 318-02) and Commentary (ACI 318R-02). Farmington Hills, MI; 2002. 1414 p

[6] Tahenni T. Etude de la capacité portante en effort tranchant des poutres en béton armé renforcées en fibres d'acier avec référence particulière aux poutres en béton à hautes performances [Doctoral Thesis]. Algiers, Algeria: University of Science and Technology Houari Boumediene; 2016. 208 p

[7] Chemrouk M. Selection of the mix constituents to produce a highly performing and durable concrete material. In: Nil Turkery A, Zengul O, editors. Paper Published in 'Durability of Building Materials and Components: Globality and Locality in Durability'; Vol. 1. Istanbul. 2008. pp. 25-32. ISBN: 978-975-561-326-0

[8] Chemrouk M, Hamrat M. High performance concrete-experimental studies of the material. In: Proceeding of the International Congress. The Challenges of Concrete Construction, Conference 1: Innovation and Development in Concrete; 2002

[9] Gutierrez PAA, Canovas MF. High performance concrete: Requirements for constituents materials and mix proportioning. ACI Materials Journal. 1996;**93**(3):233-241

[10] Malier I. Les Bétons à Haute Performance: Caractéristiques, Durabilité, et Applications. Paris: Presse de l'Ecole Nationale des Ponts et Chaussée; 1992

[11] GOM Aramis user manuel. v6. 2007. GOM mbH: Germany. Available from: http://www.gom.com [Accessed: 7 March 2019]

[12] Tahenni T, Chemrouk M, Lecompte T. Effect of steel fibers on the shear behavior of high strength concrete beams. Construction and Building Materials. 2016;**105**:14-28

[13] Tahenni T, Chemrouk M, Lecompte T. Shear behavior of high performance concrete beams using digital image correlation technique. In: Proceedings of the 4th Congrès International de Géotechnique-Ouvrage-Structures, CIGOS. 26-27 October 2017; Ho Chi Minh City, Vietnam: Lecture Notes in Civil Engineering; Vol. 8. 2018. pp. 560-570. DOI: 10.1007/978-981-10-6713-6_55

[14] Hamrat M, Boulekbache B, Chemrouk M, Amziane S. Shear behaviour of RC beams without stirrups made of normal strength and high strength concretes. Advances in Structural Engineering. 2010;**13**(1): 29-41

[15] Hamrat M, Boulekbache B, Chemrouk M, Amziane S. Effects of the transverse reinforcement on the shear behaviour of high strength concrete

beams. Advances in Structural Engineering. 2012;**15**(8):1291-1306

[16] Hamrat M. Comportement structurel du béton à hautes performances (flexion et effort tranchant) [Doctoral Thesis]. Algeria: University of Science and Technology Houari Boumediene; 2010. 143 p

[17] Taylor HPJ. The shear strength of large beams. Proceeding ASCE. 1972;**98**: 2473-2490

[18] Fenwick RC, Paulay T. Mechanisms of shear resistance of concrete beams. Journal Structure Division-ASCE. 1968; **94**:2325-2350

[19] BS 8110. Structural Use of Concrete, Part 1. Code of Practice for Design and Construction. London: British Standards Institution; 1997. 173 p

[20] Eurocode 2. Design of Concrete Structures—Part 1-1. General Rules and Rules for Buildings. EN1992-1-1,R. 2004. 100 p

[21] National Standards of New Zealand. NZS 3101—Part 1. Concrete Structures Standard. Wellington, New Zealand: Standards New Zealand; 2006

[22] Indian Standard. IS 456. Plain an reinforced concrete code of practice. (Fourth Revision); 2000. 114 p

[23] Ritter W. Schweizerische Bauzeitung (Zürich). Die Bauweise Hennebique. 1899;**33**:59-61

[24] Mörsch E. Der Eisenbetonbau, seine Anwendung und Theorie. 3ème ed. New York: MeGraw-Hill; 1902

Chapter 5

Implementation of an Artificial Vision System for Welding in the Retrofitting Process of a Robotic Arm Industrial

Yomin Estiven Jaramillo Munera, Jhon Edison Goez Mora, Juan Camilo Londoño Lopera and Edgar Mario Rico Mesa

Abstract

An industrial approach to the use of artificial vision is worked, and we are searching for the improvement of the welding process using a robotic arm. These kinds of robots in the last years have been associated to high accuracy tasks like classification, welding, object manipulation, assembly, and so on. Generally, the artificial vision is not used in works which use manipulator arm; this is normally due to the robot programmer who plans the robot task, which is executed cyclically, however, there are some approaches where different tasks using artificial vision are implemented. In this chapter, we present a retrofitting process of a manipulator welder arm Miller MR-2000, and the development of an artificial vision system, which could be used in the positioning of the machine. The developed system is able to look for areas suitable for the welding task between two pieces of material within a workspace; this process is possible using techniques of computational vision and image processing. Subsequently, the algorithm calculates the number of welding points based on the area identified previously, and finally, it sends the respective coordinates by means of G code to the robot for welding the pieces.

Keywords: robotic arm, welding system, palletizing robot, kinematics

1. Introduction

Many works related with manipulators arms have been developed since the first patent of anthropomorphic industrial robots was presented in 1973 [1]. These kinds of robot were thought to carry out a complex task in industries which represented great physical loads, or some kinds of risks for the workers. In addition, they used to be related with the search of the improvement of quality and production [2–4]. Currently, these robots have been associated to high accuracy tasks like classification, welding, object manipulation, assembly, and so on.

Artificial vision is a topic which is getting strength in the last years, which can be seen in several works where the artificial vision is used in different applications of accuracy and classification as is presented in [5, 6]. Nevertheless, the artificial vision is not constantly used in works which make developments with manipulator arms; this is normally due to the robot programmer who plans the given robot task, which is executed cyclically [7]. However, some authors present approaches where they implemented different tasks using artificial vision; an example is presented in [8], where the artificial vision is shown as an alternative to guarantee the security of the manipulator arms against collisions, instead of using sensors. On the other hand, in [9], it is shown how an object manipulator robot, which is able to distinguish between different pieces of cutlery, was designed; they divided their work in two stages: the first stage includes the recognition of the objects through computer vision algorithms and finding the coordinates of the objects; and the second stage is the realization of the movement of the robot to the found coordinates using the forward kinematic, and in addition, by means of descent gradient method. A similar approach was shown in [10], where the authors presented a prototype of a system that classifies the rocks that feed the grinding process in a concentration plant; in this case, the researchers use a 2D artificial vision system that estimates the size of the rocks based on their area and distinguishes them; nevertheless, their results are ambiguous because they did the images acquisition statically in a dynamic system.

In the case of the welding robot arms, when we can integrate technologies like artificial vision and computational intelligence with industrial robot, it is possible to adapt us to multiple environments and different types of processes, which are very attractive. The principal reason to do this implementation is to search a reduction in production times and an increase in the efficiency of the welding process. Developments as discussed earlier in this chapter take strength because most of the technologies currently available are very expensive for medium and small companies.

The aim of this chapter is to include an artificial vision system in the retrofitting robotic arm process. For this purpose, an old robot manipulator supplied by a company was used, and its behavior was checked. In the general review of the system, it was observed that it cannot make complex moves due to failures in the system, associated mainly to encoders of the servomotors. A new panel control was designed, and in addition, an open source software was implemented to integrate the welding process with artificial vision, in order to locate spatially the working pieces. In this section, the kind of robot arm, camera, and the welding system are described in a deeper way. The methodology of each stage of the project is explained, based on the robot arm kinematic and the generation of a G code with the intersection points of the pieces. A similar work as proposed in this chapter is presented in [1], where the retrofitting of an industrial robot is developed; this work is specially related with ours because the authors showed a modernization of an old robot arm, and besides, they did a comparative study related with the numerical control machines controllers integration using LinuxCNC controller and MatLab/Mach3, where they concluded that LinuxCNC is a better solution because it needs few hardware resources in comparison with Mach3/MatLab alternative; in addition, the license does not have any cost, however this work does not use artificial vision in the positioning of the tool.

2. Materials and methods

Before starting with the implementation of the artificial vision system, it was necessary to carry out a general adjustment of the robot. This process has several stages which involve hardware conditioning and considerable work in software development. The methodology addressed in this chapter is presented in **Figure 1**.

In this section, the kind of robot arm, camera, and the welding system are described in a deeper way. In addition, the methodology of the development of each stage of the project is explained.

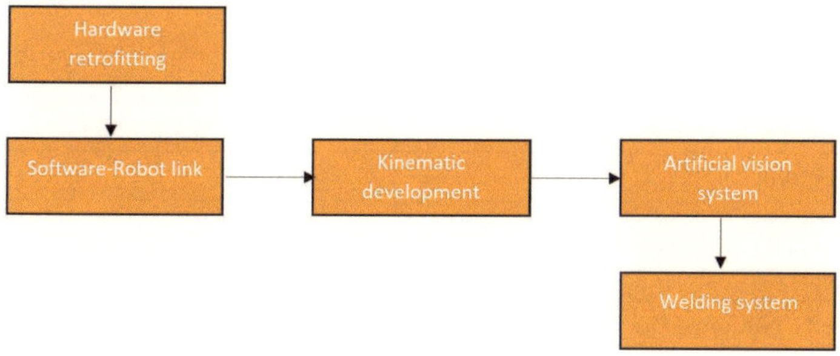

Figure 1.
Methodology description.

2.1 Robot arm

An MR-2000 welding robot Miller manufactured in 1995 is used for the development project, as shown in **Figure 2**. The robot spent several years deteriorating, and at the time of the evaluation, several errors in the motherboard and the encoders of the servomotors were found. This made impossible to use the original hardware and software.

The arm counts with a morphology of a palletizing robot, 6 freedom grades, and an approximated weight of 353 lb (160 kg). Due to the bad condition of the robot, a total rebuild of the control panel was made; for these modifications, several components were required and the most representative of them are exposed in **Table 1**.

Taking as reference the architecture of palletizing robot presented in [11], the control of the heaviest parts of the robot (base, big forward arm, and big back arm) is designed so that three servomotors of great power (1.0 kW) are responsible for global robot movements. Another three servomotors of 0.12 kW control the remaining pieces which are more focused in the final tool orientation (forearm, wrist, and a grabber). Also, the control includes computational hardware that contains the OS Linux and the vision system for the location and control of the arm.

2.2 Software-robot link

An intensive search was made for the selection of the most appropriate software for arm control; taking that into count, we realized that some of the programs in the middle are made by people who do not find a good option for this application;

Figure 2.
Welding robot Miller.

Description	Quantity
Servomotor 880-DST-A6HKB	3
Servomotor 11A-DST-A6HKB	3
DYN4-H01A2-00	3
DYN2-TLA6S-00	3
Computational Hardware	1
I25 Superport FPGA based PCI	1
Artificial vision system	1

Table 1.
Materials.

therefore, they choose to design and build their own software. These approaches have an open architecture but with much work to develop and some are unavailable.

The software used to control the robot arm is designed to CNC type machines, however, it can be implemented the kinematics of different kind of robots and all the instructions and protocols to move until a 9-Axis robot. LinuxCNC is a software widely known in robotic applications and has several advantages in respect to others [1]. It is integrated with an interface to control and monitor each move of the servomotor in a join or world mode. The software was configured using the MESA i525; this device is a general purpose FPGA based programmable I/O card for the PCI bus, and it uses standard parallel port pinouts and connectors for compatibility with most parallel port interfaced motion control/CNC breakout cards/multi-axes step motor drives; for this interface, a new parallel breakout board is designed by means of a digital optocoupled connection between the mesa 5i25 and the servodrivers; the capacitive sensor which are considered as the home switch of the robot also receives signals; this sensor is the physical mean to enable all the arm controls and has the connection of the stop control that disables the robot's hardware and software. Two of these boards are implemented, the first one for the axes 0, 1, and 2 and the other one for the axes 3, 4, and 5 distributed by the type of servodriver that drives each axis [12]. They have the compatibility to receive a numerical program (G code) for the movement of the robot, which makes possible the integration between the control of the robot and the algorithm that uses computer vision to locate the working pieces, and it generates the spacial coordinates XYZ of the welding points through a G code loaded in LinuxCNC. In order to set the MESA 5i25 for working with our electronic boards that were previously made, a custom firmware is installed in the board, where the pin inputs and pin outputs are set based on the pin distribution of our control system.

It is necessary to make the initial configuration of the machine in PNCconf of LinuxCNC, that is a helped interface which leads to user in the set up of machines which use MESA boards; however, PNCconf has several limitations from its interface, and usually, it is necessary to make modifications in the principal configuration files created by this software; those files have the *.ini* and *.hal* extensions, respectively. Normally, the modifications in the configuration files are related to the number of joint of the machine, because the interface is not possible to set more than four of them.

2.3 Kinematics development

Kinematics is a common problem in the development of software for the manipulation of the robotics arm due to math complexity. Typically, robotic arms have a setup serial where each articulation depends on the previous articulation. For the case of the robots type serial, the system can be defined by Denavit-Hartenberg parameters [13]. This approach uses homogeneous transformations by means of matrices, as this method is frequently used. Our robot is not a serial robot. The MR-2000 has a palletized [11, 14] extension that belongs to the joint 3. By this motive, it was necessary to develop a model kinematics which is able to work with that geometry.

The movements of a robotic arm are described by two types of kinematics, forward kinematics and inverse kinematics.

- *Forward kinematics*: this is a procedure to get the coordinates in our reference plane [X_T, Y_T, Z_T, A, B] taking as reference the angular positions of each joint of the system [θ_1, θ_2, θ_3, θ_4, θ_5]. This kind of kinematics is worked in LinuxCNC from joint mode.

- *Inverse kinematics*: this principally seeks to find the angular positions [θ_1, θ_2, θ_3, θ_4, θ_5] of each joint based on spatial coordinates [X_T, Y_T, Z_T, A, B] given. In this case, multiple solutions are possible. Therefore, it is quite important to define the restrictions of the robot. This kind of kinematics is worked in LinuxCNC from world mode.

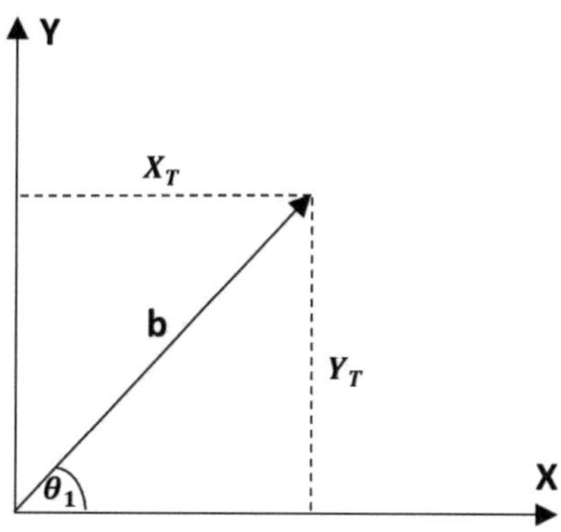

Figure 3.
Top view of the robot.

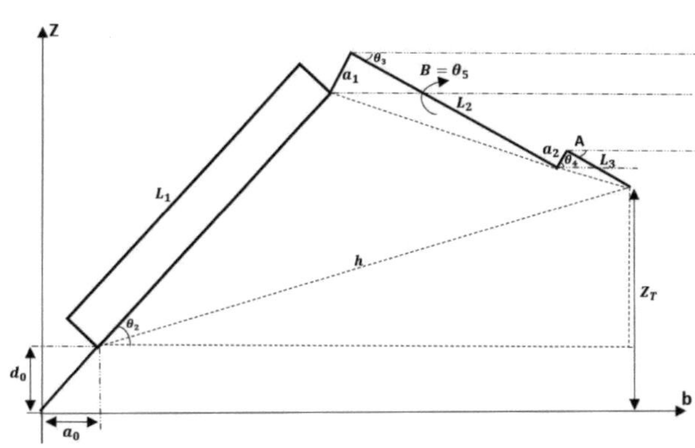

Figure 4.
Side view of the robot.

An approximation to the structure of the robot is presented in **Figures 3** and **4**, where it is possible to observe the different parameters involved in the kinematics of the robot.

LinuxCNC has a module of kinematics that allows loading a file of code C++ previously compiled with the model of the kinematics of the robot. In this file, both kinematics should be defined for the complete functioning of the robot.

2.4 Artificial vision system

The camera used is the Blackfly of 1.3 MP that has the following characteristics: resolution of 1288 × 964 px, type of CCD sensor, pixel size of 3.75 μm. This type of camera is manufactured for applications of artificial vision. It has robust features and captures precise images to contribute to the image processing stage.

3. Results

3.1 Kinematics development

In order of setting the kinematics of the robot in LinuxCNC, it is necessary to define the forward kinematics and the inverse kinematics. Therefore, it is necessary to describe mathematically both kinematics. This work is done by linking the input parameters with the output parameters with the help of geometry. The geometrical parameters (GP) of MR-2000 are shown in **Table 2**.

3.1.1 Forward kinematics

As described earlier in Section 2.3, the forward kinematics allows to find our coordinates [X_T, Y_T, Z_T, A, B] from the values of the angles of each joint, taking into count the value of the parameters [θ_1, θ_2, θ_3, θ_4, θ_5] (See **Figures 3** and **4**).

Knowing this, the coordinates are calculated as follows:

$$b = -a_1 \, sin\,(\theta_3) + L_2 \, cos\,(\theta_3) - a_2 \, sin\,(A) + L_3 \, cos\,(A) + L_1 \, cos\,(\theta_2) + a_0 \tag{1}$$

$$X_T = b * \, cos\,(\theta_1) \tag{2}$$

$$Y_T = b * \, sin\,(\theta_1) \tag{3}$$

$$Z_T = L_1 \, sin\,(\theta_2) + a_1 \, cos\,(\theta_3) + L_2 \, sin\,(\theta_3) + a_2 \, cos\,(A) + L_3 \, sin\,(A) + d_0 \tag{4}$$

$$A = \theta_3 + \theta_4 \tag{5}$$

GP of the arm	Value
a_0	300 mm
a_1	100 mm
a_2	0 mm
d_0	300 mm
L_1	500 mm
L_2	700 mm
L_3	500 mm

Table 2.
Parameters of robot.

$$B = \theta_5 \tag{6}$$

X_T and Y_T are located in **Figure 3**, and Z_T, A, and B in **Figure 4**. Based on the above, the LinuxCNC system can find the final position of the robot in the system of coordinates [X_T, Y_T, Z_T, A, B] in the joint mode.

3.1.2 Inverse kinematics

In order to find the values of angular positions based on the spatial coordinates, the following equations are developed:

$$b = \sqrt{X_T^2 + Y_T^2} \tag{7}$$

$$h = \sqrt{\left(Z_T - d_0 + \sqrt{a_2^2 + L_3^2}\, sin\left(A - arccos\left(\frac{L_3}{\sqrt{a_2^2 + L_3^2}}\right)\right)\right)^2 + (b - a_0)^2} \tag{8}$$

$$\theta_1 = arctan\left(\frac{X_T}{Y_T}\right) \tag{9}$$

$$\theta_2 = arccos\left(\frac{h^2 + L_1^2 - \sqrt{a_1^2 + L_2^2}^{\,2}}{2hL_1}\right) + arcsin\left(\frac{Z_T - d_0 + \sqrt{a_2^2 + L_3^2}\, sin\left(A - arccos\left(\frac{L_3}{\sqrt{a_2^2 + L_3^2}}\right)\right)}{h}\right) \tag{10}$$

$$\theta_3 = -\theta_2 + arccos\left(\frac{h^2 + L_1^2 - \sqrt{a_1^2 + L_2^2}^{\,2}}{2hL_1}\right) - arcsin\left(\frac{a_1}{\sqrt{a_1^2 + L_2^2}}\right) - arccos\left(\frac{\sqrt{a_1^2 + L_2^2}^{\,2} + h^2 - L_1^2}{2h\sqrt{a_1^2 + L_2^2}}\right) \tag{11}$$

$$\theta_4 = A - \theta_3 \tag{12}$$

$$\theta_5 = B \tag{13}$$

For the execution of a welding process, it is necessary that the robotic arm meets a series of requirements related to the precision and straightness in the movement of the axes. These parameters are necessary for taking the robot to work under the welding standards of parts. To verify the precision in the displacement of the axes, a dial comparator is placed as shown in **Figure 5** and the moving each axis is measured, so that the following results are obtained.

Commands by MDI (Command Line Interface) was sent to test the move of the robotic arm and the kinematics. The result of these moves is shown in the **Table 3**, where the precision of the arm is measured with a digital dial comparator with a resolution of 0.01 mm. The results show a maximum difference of 0.16 mm being permissible for the application in which it will be employed. Each axis is assembled as in **Figure 5**, in which the indicator is located parallel and centered to the axis to be measured.

Figure 5.
Digital indicator.

Displacement	Axis (X)	Axis (Y)	Axis (Z)
To 1 (mm)	0.98	0.96	0.99
To 1.5 (mm)	1.48	1.46	1.47
To 2.5 (mm)	2.46	2.45	2.47
To 5 (mm)	4.88	4.84	4.90

Table 3.
Movements.

3.2 Artificial vision system

An algorithm of computational vision is implemented in the welding process to locate spatially the pieces respect to the robot coordinates. The camera is set perpendicular to the working area at a fixed coordinate XYZAB with respect to the center robot position; the CCD makes the capture of the image that contains the pieces to be weld. OpenCV is used for the segmentation process and it is performed applying filters and morphological operation to determine the area of contact to be weld; this area becomes a straight line and the points that will be used for the creation of G code will be loaded in the numerical control.

For the processing of the images, the capture of the pieces to be weld is made, as can be seen in **Figure 6**. The working pieces are located on a surface that

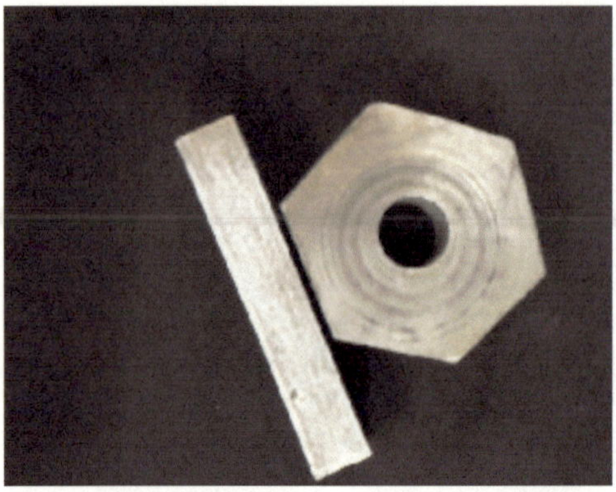

Figure 6.
Original image.

contrasts with the color of the pieces to facilitate the segmentation and identification of the edges.

Subsequently, the image is converted to a gray scale, and a Sobel filter is applied to create an image emphasizing edges. The resulting image can be observed in **Figure 7**; this process was made with the aim of being able to identify the possible closeness of the working pieces.

Before the pieces are segmented to highlight the edges, a morphological operation of closing is made to eliminate small gaps (filling them) and join components connected nearby. The kernel used is the structuring element of a rectangle of 1×8 pixels. The result is presented in **Figure 8**, where the space that separates the two pieces was totally filled.

In the last process, it is possible to highlight the suitable area for the welding process; the algorithm is able to do it due to a Gaussian filter that is applied to eliminate the rest of the edges of the piece and leave only the highlighted union of both. With the segmentation process done, the line that traces the union of the pieces is transformed into points that will be used to coordinate to which the arm must reach to carry out the welding process.

To verify the precision of the algorithm, several probes are made to check the real coordinates and the coordinates calculated from the computer vision. In this process, the values of the location of the camera and the relationship of the pixels and the location XYZAB change according to the precision of each servomotor.

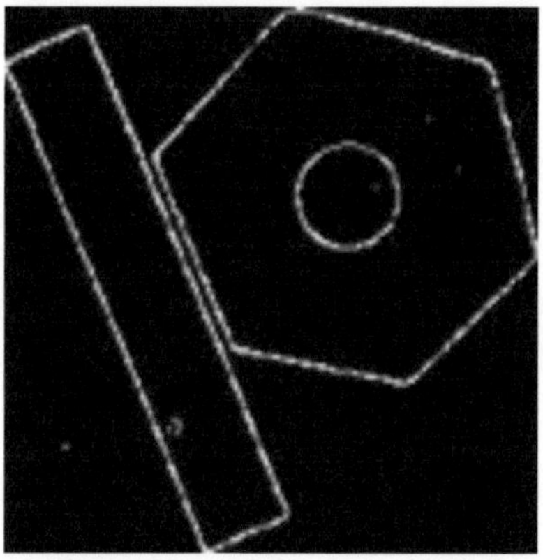

Figure 7.
Edge detection.

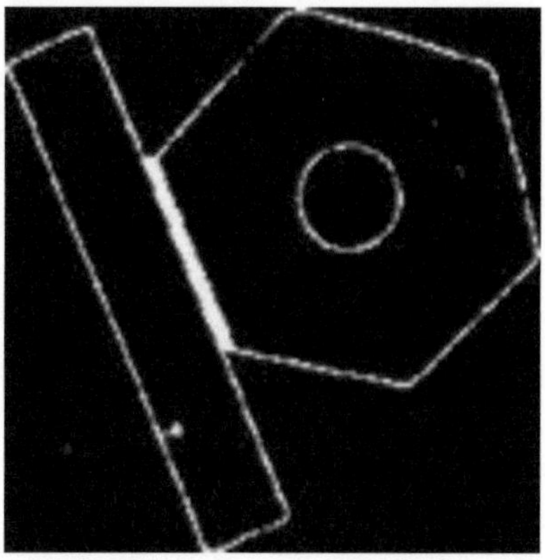

Figure 8.
Welding trajectory.

4. Conclusions

The trials show that the kinematics is the main factor that is needed for producing the natural movements of the robotic arm. Respect to the welding process, we can observe that the system achieves to be in the right standards for the development of the process. Finally, based on the results of the artificial vision phase, it is correct to say that the segmentation and edges identification process are successful, and therefore, it is possible to perform this process within the typical ranges of separation of pieces for a welding process.

Author details

Yomin Estiven Jaramillo Munera*†, Jhon Edison Goez Mora†,
Juan Camilo Londoño Lopera† and Edgar Mario Rico Mesa†
Servicio Nacional de Aprendizaje, Medellín, Colombia

*Address all correspondence to: yejaramillom@sena.edu.co

† These authors contributed equally.

References

[1] Alberto A, Eduardo J, Lima I, Marcelo H, Souza B. Retrofitting of ASEA IRB2-S6 industrial robot using numeric control technologies based on linuxcnc and MACH3-MATLAB. In: IEEE International Conference on Robotics and Biomimetics (ROBIO); Macau, China; 2017

[2] Brett PN, Khodabandehloo K. Analysis of bi-arm robots for applications in manufacturing industry. Proceedings of the Institution of Mechanical Engineers. Part B: Journal of Engineering Manufacture. 1991;**205**: 43-50. DOI: 10.1243/PIME

[3] Wehe DK, Lee JC, Martin WR. Intelligent robotics and remote systems for the nuclear industry. Nuclear Engineering and Design. Department of Nuclear Engineering, University of Michigan. 1989;**113**:259-267

[4] Neda A, Ali L. Socialization of industrial robots: An innovative solution to improve productivity. In: 9th Annual Information Technology, Electronics and Mobile Communication Conference (IEMCON); Vancouver, Canada. IEEE; 2018. pp. 832-837

[5] Londono Lopera JC, Goez Mora JE, Rico Mesa EM. Positioning of the Cutting Tool of a CNC Type Milling Machine by Means of Digital Image Processing Advances in Computing. CCC 2018. Communications in Computer and Information Science. Vol. 885. Cham: Springer;

[6] Goez Mora JE, Londono Lopera JC, Patino Cortes DA. Automatic Visual Classification of Parking Lot Spaces: A Comparison Between BoF and CNN Approaches. Applied Computer Sciences in Engineering. WEA 2018. Communications in Computer and Information Science. Vol. 915. Cham: Springer;

[7] Frank C. Programming vision-guided industrial robot operations. Journal of Engineering Technology;**3009**(26):10-15

[8] Fevery B, Wyns B, Boullart L. Industrial robot manipulator guarding using artificial vision. In: Robot Vision. Vol. 28. Rijeka, Croatia: IntechOpen; 2006. DOI: 10.5772/9294

[9] Bilal I, Huseyin A, Yakup K, Serdar Y, Yildirim E. Smart robot arm motion using computer vision. Elektronika Ir Elektotechnika. 2015;**21**(6):3-7

[10] Rene V, Aldo C. System for classifying rocks by using artificial vision and a robot arm. In: ISIE '97 Proceeding of the IEEE International Symposium on Industrial Electronics; July 7–11, 1997. Guimaraes, Portugal: IEEE; 1997

[11] Yong T, Fang C, Hegen X. Kinematics and workspace of a 4-DOF hybrid palletizing robot. Advances in Mechanical Engineering. 2014;**6**:1-6

[12] 5I25 Picture, MESA Electronics [Internet]. Available from: http://store.mesanet.com/index.php?route=product/product&product_id=55 [Accessed: 27 March 2019]

[13] Corke P. A simple and systematic approach to assigning a simple and systematic approach to assigning. IEEE Transactions on Robotics. 2007;**23**: 590-594

[14] Rui Z, Zhou B, Liu J. Dynamic simulation of palletizing robots based on ADAMS. In: 2nd International Conference on Electronic & Mechanical Engineering and Information Technology; Lanzhou, China; 2012. pp. 1446-1449

Chapter 6

EBSCO Discovery Service (EDS) Usage in Israeli Academic Libraries

Riki Greenberg

Abstract

Awareness to the problem that different search interfaces discourage patrons' use of library information sources has led academic libraries to implement web-scale discovery services. These services offer the user a "Google-like" search experience of library resources. This study aims to explore library professionals' satisfaction, patrons' information behavior, and use of EDS discovery tool service in academic libraries in Israel. Mixed research methods were used in this study: qualitative and quantitative. Qualitative research methods are through content analysis of library directors' interviews, and quantitative research method is through collected library metrics (from Google analytics) data analysis, regarding usage patterns and search session analysis. The study aims to gain insight regarding library implementation and patrons' information behavior of the EDS discovery tool, in Israeli higher education institutions.

Keywords: information behavior, academic libraries, Israel, EDS discovery service, search in the library

1. Introduction

Academic libraries are committed to providing their patrons with an easy and intuitive search experience, similar to what they expect from their favorite search engine, Google. Discovery services have an important role in revealing the library's collection to its users. These tools reduce time and effort spent in both searching and learning to use the various database interfaces. A query from one search box produces a list of organized results for the user to review. Assessing user information behavior and librarians' feedback are crucial for improving these services and presenting library patrons with a better user experience.

2. Information search in libraries

User expectations for library resources have changed dramatically; individuals have become too impatient to search in multiple databases to access desired information. Library patrons are challenged by alternate search interfaces that can discourage the full use of the given resources. Information overload has become another issue; users have online access to a variety of subscribed databases, but they have limited understanding of what they are and how to use them. Therefore, librarians are actively seeking better ways to integrate and present information [1].

Searching for sources in the library cannot be discussed without addressing the impact of the Google search engine. Google has become a powerful presence in the life of all library users. It is the most popular search engine for queries about daily issues and for academic needs. It empowers library visitors to search for their academic information needs, within an easy and popular interface [2]. In libraries, some consider this an obstacle, and some see it as an opportunity for innovations and improvements. One thing is certain: Google redefined the search experience, and libraries should acknowledge this.

In 2004, Google launched Google Scholar, a tool for discovering scholarly information. Google Scholar is a search engine for academic articles, theses, books, abstracts, and court opinions from academic publishers, professional societies, online repositories, universities, and other websites. This free resource, with its basic and familiar interface, has the potential to serve as a scholarly metasearch information engine [3, 4]. Google Scholar has received mixed receptions from the librarian community. It has some advanced search features, but it provides no interface for refining the results. Users can set preferences such as language, year, author, and periodical title. They can also view an indication of the libraries from which it can access the source, citation export options, and how to cite the source (for many citation styles). The reviews and critiques of Google Scholar have been mixed, at best. Its content, its search engine, its interface, and its citation count have all been criticized. Patrons of libraries who have subscriptions to the digital archives of publishers are the greatest beneficiaries of Google Scholar, as with a single search they are led to the full digital text versions of the articles [4–6]. Google Scholar is very different from library database interfaces and their search options, yet it introduces library users to scholarly articles through a familiar and friendly interface.

3. Discovery tools

Discovery services are vital tools to increase search ability and accessibility of library resources. A combined search interface for multiple resources will help users discover relevant content. The tool reduces time and effort spent in both searching and learning to use the various database interfaces. It broadcasts a query across all sources and returns one organized list of results for the user [7, 8]. Discovery services have become almost essential in academic libraries. The libraries need to create a discovery layer that simplifies the search process while broadening the richness of resources availability in a Google-like interface. The discovery service is comprised of pre-indexed materials from many library information sources. The discovery solution enables faceted browsing, relevance ranking, and limitation options to refine the search results. Discovery tool services are the libraries' attempt to offer a "Google-like" search experience of library resources.

The discovery tool makes it possible to create a centralized index of an institution's information resources through a single point of access. Since the content is pre-indexed, response time is very quick and meets the user's needs. Discovery tools enable to connect patrons with the library's storehouse of information and search indexes and databases quickly and easily. These tools tend to be more popular with users, especially undergraduates, than traditional library search tools [9–12].

Libraries took upon themselves to review current web-scale discovery solutions and implement it accordingly. In their review, Karadia and Pati [13] suggest a summary of discovery tools' advantages:

i. Connect users with the content from different sources

ii. Quick search across a vast number of resources in a one-stop search box

iii. Relevancy-ranked results in an intuitive interface expected by today's information seekers

iv. Simplify the research process

v. Increase the use of library resources

As Hanrath and Kottman [14] summarize, there is a wide consensus in the literature that discovery tools are one way of retaining patrons who are already immersed in the "world of Google" and to bring them back to the library world.

In this work, we present a case study of six academic libraries in Israel, who chose to implement EBSCO Discovery Service (EDS).

4. Study population

Education is highly valued within Israel's national culture, and its higher education sector has been acknowledged for helping to encourage the country's development. There are nine universities in Israel, as well as numerous higher education colleges. Courses are often taught in Hebrew, though Israeli universities also offer English-taught programs. In Israel, academic libraries started to implement discovery services in 2010 [9].

This study uses data from three governmental universities and three colleges (two governmental and one private), to reflect on information behavior and discovery tool use in different types of users and institutions. Every library in our study is unique, each with a diverse organizational culture, a distinct student population, and different educational programs and specialties. This enables us to draw a representation of academic library users in Israel.

5. Methodology

The study uses a mixed-methods approach to gather both quantitative and qualitative data on usage of EDS discovery service tool. We analyzed librarians' interviews regarding their professional perspectives and patrons search information behavior via Google analytics transaction logs to reveal interactions between users and the discovery system.

6. Findings and discussion

6.1 Qualitative research method

We contacted 10 academic library directors, according to a given list of Israeli libraries that implemented the EDS service (at least 2 years ago). The contact was made via email, which asked them to participate in the study; six of which accepted. We conducted an hour-long interview by phone or by face-to-face meetings, with each library director (two of which, referred us to the head of the discovery tool services in the library). We discussed three topics: the decision procedure, the essence of EDS discovery tool, and the search behavior of the library patrons. The questions were regarding their professional practice, general philosophies, and opinion.

6.1.1 Reasons for choosing EDS

Libraries based their choice to implement EDS discovery tool on peers' recommendations, joint committee discussions, and literature reviews. Massive library and information science (LIS) sources deal with issues regarding planning, choosing and implementing discovery tools. Librarians are exposed to information made available through peer-reviewed papers, presentations, and online discussions in various platforms (national and international). In her book *Planning and Implementing Resource Discovery Tools in Academic Libraries*, Mary Pagliero Popp [15] suggests that there is a framework for evaluating discovery tools. This framework discusses involving library staff from various libraries and asking them for their technical and functional experience. There is also a thorough review on selected features and best practice for the evaluation and the selection procedure.

According to the interviewees, the main reasons for choosing EDS were the ease of use and the Google-like interface. Shi and Levy [16] determined that EBSCO Discovery Services is one of the discovery search tools that is highly recommended by librarians. In her work on maximizing academic libraries' collections use, Kristine Calvert [17] declares that EDS presents a simplified search experience through a single search box, which exposes a far greater number of the library's resources. In their study, Thompson and her colleagues [18] studied the results of George Washington university library staff's focus group. The study was conducted to assess user satisfaction with EDS service, and it found that librarians like the familiar EBSCO host-type interface as their discovery tool search box.

The quality of metadata was another reason mentioned in the interviews and the fact that EBSCO is also the vendor of their most popular databases. Therefore, the librarians believed the service would reflect the same professional advantages. As mentioned in the literature, EBSCO has a solid reputation for their comprehensive collection of content, sophisticated search options, and responsive technical support. Kristine Calvert [17] studied the Western Carolina University library decision to use EDS discovery tool service. In her findings, she suggests that the preference for EBSCO's products was based on two primary reasons. First, West Carolina University library has subscription to a large number of databases on the EBSCOhost platform, therefore wanting to maximize use of those databases, and second, the confidence the library has in the product relevancy rankings.

Two of the librarians in the study did a cross search to compare relevancy of results in three available discovery tools and found EDS to have the highest result relevancy. In the literature there is not a definitive answer on which discovery tool produces the higher relevancy results. In their study, Shi and Levy [16] review EDS advantages in performing a smart search. They found that the service leads users to adequate results as well as offering suggested adjustments by narrowing or limiting the information sources retrieved in search. In a survey named "Librarian Assessment of the Quality and Relevance of Search Results" conducted by librarians at the Cornell University library [19], the responders ranked EDS as better in its interface and in its ease of use. As for the search results, EDS appears to work better only for some disciplines (compared to Summon). Asher, Duke, and Wilson [3] studied the ability of students to locate information resources, which indicated better results for the students using EBSCO Discovery Service.

6.1.2 First choice of search tool

All the interviewees thought that Google Scholar was and still is the student's first and primary choice. The fact that it is well-known and familiar to most of them makes it the preferable search interface. This fact is well supported by the literature;

Google Scholar receives higher usability and preference ratings from students because it is easy to access, convenient, easy to use, and fast [20–24]. They always prefer Google Scholar to library databases and discovery tools.

Interviewees mentioned the fact that libraries need to keep cooperating with Google Scholar and enable access to its subscriptions. Patrons of libraries, who have subscriptions to the digital archives of publishers, are the greatest beneficiaries of the Google Scholar services. With a single search, they are led to the full digital text of the requested item [6]. In their research, Dempsey and Malpas [25] studied the future of the academic library in the context of diversity and change. They suggest that library users have lost their track on content supply. There is an increasing overlap between library and Google Scholar in workflow and network identity when they disclose and share information sources.

Most library directors mentioned Google Scholar and EDS as part of the same instruction meetings for research students. Hanneke and O'Brien [26] found that while librarians always hope for the opportunity to provide instruction on advanced searching, students and faculty could successfully use discovery tools to perform a research process. Therefore, searching instruction is either not available or not desired. Contradicting their results, other studies [27] have found that information search interfaces including Google Scholar and discovery tools very often retrieve a large number of records in response to a simple query, which requires search expertise to manipulate the results to find adequate information. Users need librarian's guidance in order to find and retrieve information.

Another topic that arose from the study was regarding search results. According to the interviewees, the EDS system provides fewer but better results than Google Scholar. This is supported by the literature; Karen Ciccone and John Vickery from North Carolina State University Libraries [28] found that there was no significant difference in the results between Summon and EDS, for either known item or topical searches. They also found that the higher proficiency of students using EDS leads to higher quality academic resources. However, Google Scholar outperformed both discovery services, in topical searches.

The librarians recommend EDS to their students, and it is referred to as the library's "Google Scholar." Asher, Duke, and Wilson [3] well described it in their work *Paths of Discovery* when they review the advantages of discovery tools:

Providing a uniform search interface and aggregating content behind a single "brand," discovery tools like EDS, Summon, and GS help to diminish the "cognitive load" on students by eliminating the often difficult and confusing step of choosing an appropriate disciplinary database, as well as the need to repeat searches in multiple databases.

6.1.3 Coverage, relevance of results, and ease of use

Ease of use was the most popular motive in all the interviews. The fact that students do not need to learn how to use new database interfaces makes it much easier on the library clients. Studies of information seeking behavior indicate that users act according to the principle of least effort and ease of use [29]. Students also tend to minimize their effort at the expense of the quality of their results. Information sources that are found quickest and easiest are those that are most likely to be used by students [3].

All the library's directors mentioned examining usage statistics to ensure that the tool is highly used among the patrons. In the literature, we find that libraries must monitor their service efficiency by aggregating data from all available sources [20]. In his work, *The Future of Library Resource Discovery*, Marshall Breeding [30] discusses the considerable interest of libraries in the ability to measure the performance of their discovery service. He suggests that patron's information behavior should be recorded and evaluated for the improvement of user experience and service.

Four out of six libraries use EDS solely for publishers' subscriptions. Their intention was to extend usage of the E-journals subscriptions and to enable their patrons to find and retrieve full-text articles. This notion is well supported in the literature. In her work, *Maximizing Academic Library Collections: Measuring Changes in Use Patterns Owing to EBSCO Discovery Service*, Kristin Calvert from the University of North Carolina's library [17] found that EDS discovery tool had a strong positive effect on E-journal use. Additionally, it appears to maximize the value of library subscriptions. Thompson and her collogues [18] support these findings; according to their study, EDS has changed user behavior to better connect users to the library's E-journal collection and increases use of full text and abstracts, especially in the EBSCO host databases.

All the study participants indicated the quality of results, quality of the search algorithm, and quality of metadata as factors that enable high-precision search. Marshall Breeding [30] indicated that discovery tool interfaces include features such as relevancy-based search results, faceted navigation, and presentation of search results listed either in a brief form or in full-record displays. Studies have also proven that discovery systems generally support better relevancy rankings and deliver higher quality resources [1, 3, 18].

All interviewees mentioned the good customer relations they have with EBSCO representatives. The transparency, the flexibility of the system, and the responsiveness of the support team add to their positive user experience. In his report on index-based discovery services from 2018, Marshall Breeding [31] writes that EBSCO Discovery Service success among libraries is due to its interoperability with strategic systems implemented in libraries, its content coverage, and its interface design.

One of the interviewees referred to EDS as a starting and more general search point, primarily for bachelor's degree students. In her opinion, research students prefer a more accurate search in their native databases. Thompson and her colleagues [18] found that students like the EDS search interface and frequented it, because of prior successful searches. Asher et al. [3] found that student's search strategies use simple keyword searches, as they do in Google. They also feel that they could get access to full-text resources more quickly and easily.

Two university library directors specified that in the fields of social sciences and humanities, the system produces good results but less so in the exact sciences. McCracken and her colleagues at Cornell university library [19] also found that EDS appears to produce better and more accurate search results, only for some disciplines (in comparison to other discovery tools available).

One of the library directors mentioned a specific case in which the university had a few hours of technical difficulties. During which, she received many complaints from faculty and students on the unavailability of the service. This is well supported in studies that indicate the popularity of the discovery tool search interface for library patrons [3, 18].

Three of the interviewees declared that the reference librarians use "native databases" for economic, business, and legal data. In her work on librarian's search preferences, Foster [32] found that when helping patrons, librarians choose web-scale discovery systems or subject-specific databases as starting point of the search. When librarians preform an independent search, they prefer only subject-specific databases as their chosen starting point.

6.1.4 Access point

All libraries use EDS search box in the main menu of the library home page. Two of the interviewees indicated that they choose to include a tab in the search box for native databases and a separate tab for the EDS service. The other four interviewees used the EDS service as their default search tab for English articles. The libraries' goal is to improve the accessibility and visibility of its online resources while providing user experience shaped through consultation and engagement. In his work on improving access to e-resources for users at the University of Derby, Kay [33] describes the planning and designing of the EDS discovery search box. He reviews the process made up of a few stages: first, student's feedback on what kind of search tab they would prefer, and second, the library presented a selection of potential icon designs and asked them to choose their favorites. The same procedure was made for library staff from different services. The implementation staff also met with EBSCO representatives to become familiar with the best practices at other institutions. As a result, they designed a bigger search box with a more dynamic look and brighter color scheme.

In our study, all participants indicated concern regarding too many results per search. Some activated only subscripted periodical archives while eliminating open access and other articles. They also commented that keyword search is the most common and popular search among their patrons. The literature indicates [10, 34, 35] that a careful evaluation needs to be made on which settings and customization of the discovery tool will best serve the students. Since these settings will affect their search results and research outcomes, students will use basic search functionality and usually rely on the first page of search results due to their trust in the algorithm relevancy rankings. By structuring and ordering the way information is presented, libraries can influence their user's information behavior.

The librarians believe that students use EDS without any instruction, just click and go. The literature on this points out that librarians need to reevaluate instructions at the reference desk and in the classroom. Instructions can be used to teach patrons basic search skills, allowing more time to focus on research skills and encourages them to evaluate the information [35, 36].

All the participants declared that EDS is the portal for full-text search. If the patron does not have access to a link to the full article, in their opinion the service does not meet the expectations. Therefore, the link resolver has to be precise and as transparent as possible to the end user. This finding matches Marshall Breeding's work on the future of library resource discovery [30]. He characterizes the discovery tool interface as interoperable with a link resolver, to present links to full text from citation records in search results.

Libraries have adopted web-scale discovery services as one-stop research shops over the past years. Studies report that users find it easy of use and that it produces better search results with high-quality resources. To complete librarians' interviews and to learn more about the users' point of view, we have to analyze and understand their interactions with EDS. The usage data and log files analyses are extremely useful and valuable for libraries, in order to reveal the user's information behavior. It can also indicate how the library can implement this for a better and successful experience with its information resources.

6.2 Quantitative research method

Every action that a user does is recorded and represents the way he or she uses the discovery tool. The study uses data mining from Google Analytics platform, monitoring all the involved libraries. We implemented an automatically generated tracking code to record every EDS page generated, on basic and advanced search screens and search result pages. The study reviewed reports regarding information behavior and technology metrics. Reports were generated in Google Analytics and exported as Microsoft Excel spreadsheets. The Excel spreadsheets provided the ability to sort searches for more detailed data analysis.

The data was collected during the first semester of the 2018–2019 academic year, from December to January.

Terragni and Hassani [37] found that there are some limitations in Google analytics data analyses:

1. No indication about which user made a particular choice.

2. The system cannot provide end-to-end process maps that can show and explain choices and loops between activities.

3. There is no analysis of the processes from different perspectives (e.g., time constraints, bottlenecks, or relations between resources).

However, we chose this platform in order to gain an overall idea of how the library patrons behave, to compare this behavior with what library professionals expected, and to make the user experience more efficient and successful.

6.2.1 Usage patterns

On average, a single user preforms two sessions. Session duration is 11 min, and every user uses eight pages per session. The average session duration is impressively high, since we find that studies report on session search duration of 5 min [38] or even shorter duration of 3.46 min [17]. We may assume that this is because Israeli students are mostly native Hebrew speakers and use English mostly for academic and spoken language. Because of this, they might require extra time to linguistically decode the research items they find [20].

6.2.2 Devices

Most patrons (93%) use EDS from their desktop computers, 4.14% are mobile users, and less than 1% use tablets. The data resembles the Cohen and Thorpe study [39] on EDS usage statistics in two Indiana University campuses. They found that 98% of the discovery tool visitors were desktop users (PC and laptops). This indicates that EDS visitors mainly use desktops for their information searches. In their work, Chang and Liu [40]) discuss how mobile use of the Internet is gradually changing people's information behavior. They studied mobile application reading sessions and suggest four stages model for mobile user interaction: (i) accessing the applications, (ii) searching for the content, (iii) reading, and (iv) interacting. It would be interesting to further study, check, and characterize mobile usage of discovery tools and determine why it is relatively low according to our research data. This study clearly demonstrates that EDS is not one of the patron's preferred mobile applications. Therefore, libraries must assess and improve the EDS mobile user experience.

6.2.3 Users' information behavior

On average, 65.48% of the total users turn to the basic search box as their starting point of access (first interaction data (see **Figure 1**)). In all six libraries, the default page on EDS is the basic search page. Users must intentionally navigate to the advanced search page, so most of them will use the default and basic search box. When students use the discovery service, they type a few relevant keywords, which enable them to find rich, fast, and ranked search results [36]. Asher et al. [4] also found that students usually trust the search engine's algorithms. They trust

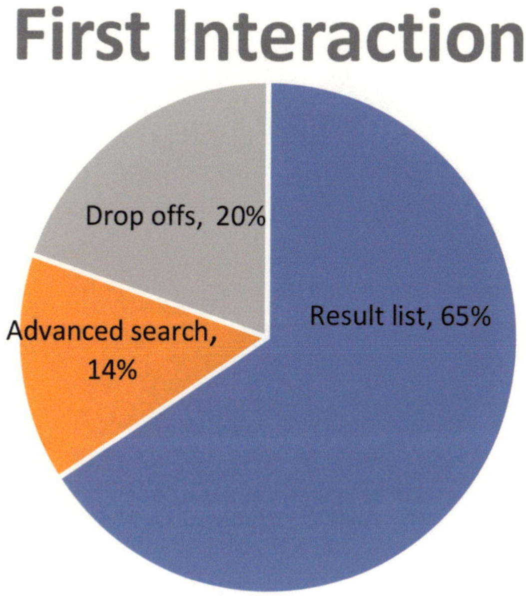

Figure 1.
First interaction behavior flow (Participants that dropped out were not included in the analysis).

its relevancy ranking and are satisfied with its results. Calvert [17] suggests that if users find something sufficient for their information needs, they will use that resource instead of seeking a better one.

On average, 14.42% of the total users turn to the advanced search box as their starting point of access (first interaction data (see **Figure 1**)). In their work on discovery services usage at Indiana University, Meg Galasso and her colleagues [36] found that although librarians assumed discovery tools were intuitive and easy to use, many users are not using it effectively. This small percentage of users indicates that they find the basic search interface inadequate for their needs. It can also indicate that users act according to the principle of least effort and ease of use [29]. In her work *Millennial Students' Mental Models of Search*, Holman [41] found that most students prefer simple searches even if they retrieve a larger quantity of results. Studies also found that unlike undergraduates, more experienced students are already familiar with focusing their search and make use of the advanced search features of the discovery tool. Navigation to this option suggests a deeper level of understanding and a more sophisticated research processes [42]. In their work *Discovering User Behavior*, Cohen and Thorpe [39] suggest to characterize discovery service users as either light users or heavy users. The heavy users should be taught advanced searching techniques for their information needs. While this study observed users search behavior, it would prove useful for further study of different types of user's information behavior (undergraduates, graduates, doctoral students, and faculty) while conducting their research assignments.

On average, 49.28% of the total users entered the details of their bibliographic records as their second interaction with EDS (see **Figure 2**). We can assume that these patrons find the search results adequate for their information needs. We can also assume that clicking on the full-record option enables patrons to check if the item matches or exceeds their expectation. In her work, Calvert [17] found that academic users read the abstracts in order to judge the relevancy of the specific information source, prior to accessing the full text. She also found that patrons avoid additional result pages; they are likely to access only six detailed records in a result list before leaving the search service or modifying the search. Cassidy and her

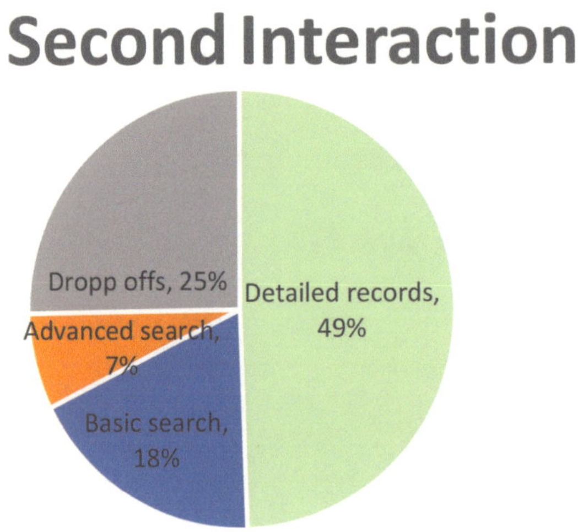

Figure 2.
Second interaction behavior flow (Participants that dropped out were not included in the analysis).

colleagues [34] found that the majority of students would not click on additional result pages. They expect the discovery tool to retrieve the most relevant information items on the first page and therefore checking the detailed relevant records and accordingly accessing the full text.

On average, 17.67% of the total users decided to preform another search using the basic search dialog box as their second interaction with EDS (see **Figure 2**). This small percentage of users was seemingly not satisfied by their initial search results. From this study data analysis, we cannot ascertain the exact reason these users choose to leave the current search and preform an alternate one. It is important to specify that these users did not choose an advanced search box to modify their preliminary search; they simply restarted their search on the basic search box. The reason for this might be a poor choice of keywords, misspelling, looking for a specific item, or inadequate search results. Cassidy and her colleagues [34] also suggest that students are more likely to modify a search than to proceed through a number of result pages.

On average, 7% of the total users decided to continue and refine their search strategy through the advanced search dialog box as their second interaction (see **Figure 2**). As mentioned in the literature review, patrons tend to adopt a simple search string and consider themselves both successful and satisfied with the results. Therefore, what is found most quickly and easily is often most likely to be used [34, 41]. In this study, 7% of the users choose differently; thus, we assume they found that the results did not meet their expectations. This may be due to an information overload or too many results in their first interaction, which caused them to narrow down the search, via advanced search. In his work on discovery tools and information overload, Shapiro [35] claims that libraries expect their discovery services to simplify the search process for their clients. In practice, it did not simplify the task of conducting research nor did it ease the patrons' information overload. Calvert [17] summarizes that library patrons use the discovery service as they would use Google. This may result in an unproductive search, which in our study lead experienced patrons to reuse the discovery service in a more efficient matter, through the advanced search option.

7. Summary and conclusion

This study sought to bring a broad overview of EDS discovery service use in Israeli academic libraries by analyzing librarian's interviews and Google Analytics usage data. Here are the main focal points of the research: the main reasons for choosing EDS platform by the Israeli libraries were high relevancy, quality of metadata, and ease of use. According to the librarians, Google Scholar is the first choice of library users. In all participating libraries, EDS is the default search tab for non-Hebrew articles. All the libraries in the study used the basic search box as the default interface. The librarians thought that only a minority of users would use the advanced search box options. According to Google Analytics data, each user performs on average two sessions, with an average duration of 11 minutes. The vast majority (93%) of patrons use EDS service from their desktop. Most patrons (65.48%) use the basic search box as their starting point, while 14.42% of total users first use the advanced search.

In their second interaction, most patrons (49.28%) entered the details of the bibliographic records. Some (17.67%) decided to preform another search using the basic search box. Only 7% of the total users decided to continue and refine their search through the advanced search dialog box.

8. Recommendations

The study findings reveal user behavior trends, which may be implemented for a better understanding of the usage of EDS and may encourage libraries to develop strategies to improve instruction techniques, as well as discovery service interface enhancements. Further studies need to investigate specific information behavior of different user populations (undergraduate, faculty, and advanced users). It is important to study further the pros and cons of the service in light of usability testing.

Acknowledgements

The author wishes to thank EBSCO for supporting this research.

The author also wishes to thank the institutions' library directors, for their cooperation and willingness to share their thoughts and data with the author.

Appendix

Library administrators' interview questionnaire regarding EDS (EBSCO Discovery Services).

Demographic details:

Name of University/College ______________________________.
× Governmental.
× Private.
Name of library____________________________________.
Job Title____________________________________.

Interview Questions:

1. Reasons for choosing EDS

2. Students' first choice of search tool

3. Coverage, relevance of results, and ease of use

4. Access point

Comments and questions:
____.
____.
____.
____.
____.
____.
____.
____.
____.

Author details

Riki Greenberg
University of Haifa Library, Haifa, Israel

*Address all correspondence to: riki@univ.haifa.ac.il

References

[1] Allison D, Mering M. Use of discovery tools in ARL libraries. Faculty Publications, UNL Libraries. 2018. p. 366. Available from: https://digitalcommons.unl.edu/libraryscience/366 [Accessed: 15 August 2019]

[2] Miller W, Pellen RM. Libraries and Google. New York: Routledge; 2014

[3] Asher AD, Duke LM, Wilson S. Paths of discovery: Comparing the search effectiveness of EBSCO discovery service, summon, Google Scholar, and conventional library resources. College & Research Libraries. 2013;**74**(5):464-488

[4] Neuhaus C, Neuhaus E, Asher A. Google Scholar goes to school: The presence of Google Scholar on college and university web sites. The Journal of Academic Librarianship. 2008;**34**(1):39-51

[5] Jacsó P. Google Scholar: The pros and the cons. Online Information Review. 2005;**29**(2):208-214

[6] Pomerantz J. Google Scholar and 100 percent availability of information. Information Technology and Libraries. 2006;**25**(2):52-56

[7] Ellero NP. Integration or disintegration: Where is discovery headed? Journal of Library Metadata. 2013;**13**(4):311-329

[8] Wang Y, Mi J. Searchability and discoverability of library resources: Federated search and beyond. College & Undergraduate Libraries. 2012;**19**(2-4):229-245

[9] Aharony N, Prebor G. Librarians' and information professionals' perspectives towards discovery tools—An exploratory study. The Journal of Academic Librarianship. 2015;**41**(4):429-440

[10] De Smet E, Dhamdhere S, editors. E-discovery tools and applications in modern libraries. In: IGI Global. 2016

[11] Durante K, Wang Z. Creating an actionable assessment framework for discovery services in academic libraries. College & Undergraduate Libraries. 2012;**19**(2-4):215-228

[12] Spencer JS, Millson-Martula C. Discovery Tools: The Next Generation of Library Research. Routledge; 2016

[13] Karadia S, Pati A. Discovery tools and services for academic libraries. In: 2015 1st National Conference on Next Generation Librarianship. Gujarat, India: C.U. Shah University. pp. 135-140

[14] Hanrath S, Kottman M. Use and usability of a discovery tool in an academic library. Journal of Web Librarianship. 2015;**9**(1):1-21

[15] Popp MP, editor. Planning and implementing resource discovery tools in academic libraries. In: IGI Global. 2012

[16] Shi X, Levy S. An empirical review of library discovery tools. Journal of Service Science and Management. 2015;**8**(05):716

[17] Calvert K. Maximizing academic library collections: Measuring changes in use patterns owing to EBSCO discovery service. College & Research Libraries. 2015;**76**(1):81-99

[18] Thompson JL, Sullo E, Abate LE, Heselden M, Lyons KM. Discovery assessment and improvement at an academic health sciences library: Health information@ Himmelfarb five years later. Journal of Electronic Resources in Medical Libraries. 2018;**15**(1):7-25

[19] McCracken P, Chandler A, Koennecke J, Mobley L, Thitchener L,

Wright SJ, et al. User services and technical services analysis of ex libris vs EBSCO discovery layer and electronic resources management tools. 2019. Available from: ecommons.cornell.edu. [Accessed: 15 August 2019]

[20] Greenberg R. Academic information behavior and the role of the academic library: A study of an Israeli university [doctoral dissertation]. 2016. Available from: Thesiscommons.org. [Accessed: 15 August 2019]

[21] Greenberg R, Bar-Ilan J. Information needs of students in Israel—A case study of a multicultural society. The Journal of Academic Librarianship. 2014;**40**(2):185-191

[22] Delaney G, Bates J. How can the university library better meet the information needs of research students? Experiences from Ulster University. New Review of Academic Librarianship. 2018;**24**(1):63-89

[23] Wu MD, Chen SC. Graduate students appreciate Google scholar, but still find use for libraries. The Electronic Library. 2014;**32**(3):375-389

[24] Zhang T. User-centered evaluation of a discovery layer system with Google Scholar. In: International Conference of Design, User Experience, and Usability. Springer; 2013. pp. 313-322

[25] Dempsey L, Malpas C. Academic library futures in a diversified university system. In: Gleason N, editor. Higher Education in the Era of the Fourth Industrial Revolution. Singapore: Palgrave Macmillan; 2018

[26] Hanneke R, O'Brien KK. Comparison of three web-scale discovery services for health sciences research. Journal of the Medical Library Association: JMLA. 2016;**104**(2):109

[27] Bandyopadhyay A, Boyd-Byrnes MK. Is the need for mediated reference service in academic libraries fading away in the digital environment? Reference Services Review. 2016;**44**(4):596-626

[28] Ciccone K, Vickery J. Summon, EBSCO discovery service, and Google Scholar: A comparison of search performance using user queries. Evidence Based Library and Information Practice. 2015;**10**(1):34-49

[29] Colon-Aguirre M, Freberg K, Allard S. Perceptions and uses of Google Scholar among undergraduate students. In: Paper Presented at the “Science Communication and Information Research” 33rd Annual Research Symposium College of Communication and Information. Knoxville, TN: The University of Tennessee; 2011

[30] Breeding M. The future of library resource discovery. Information Standards Quarterly. 2015;**27**(1):24-30

[31] Breeding M. Index-based discovery services: Current players and products. Library Technology Reports. 2018;**54**(8):12

[32] Foster AK. Determining librarian research preferences: A comparison survey of web-scale discovery systems and subject databases. The Journal of Academic Librarianship. 2018;**44**(3):330-336

[33] Kay J. Improving Access to e-Resources for Users at the University of Derby: Enhancing Discovery Systems with Library Plus 2.0. Insights. Vol. 32. 2019. p. 1

[34] Cassidy ED, Jones G, McMain L, Shen L, Vieira S. Student searching with EBSCO discovery: A usability study. Journal of Electronic Resources Librarianship. 2014;**26**(1):17-35

[35] Shapiro S. Academic librarians, information overload, and the Tao of

discovery. The Journal of Academic Librarianship. 2018;**44**(5):671-673

[36] Galasso M, Cohen RA, Thorpe Pusnik A. A cascading approach to training discovery. Reference Services Review. 2019;**47**(1):60-72

[37] Terragni A, Hassani M. Analyzing customer journey with process mining: From discovery to recommendations. In: 2018 IEEE 6th International Conference on Future Internet of Things and Cloud (FiCloud). IEEE; 2018. pp. 224-229

[38] Allison D. OAI-PMH harvested collections and user engagement. Journal of Web Librarianship. 2016;**10**(1):14-27

[39] Cohen RA, Thorpe A. Discovering user behavior: Applying usage statistics to shape frontline services. The Serials Librarian. 2015;**69**(1):29-46

[40] Chang Y, Liu F. Network traffic and user behavior analysis of mobile reading applications. In: 2016 Sixth International Conference on Information Science and Technology (ICIST). IEEE; 2016. pp. 142-146

[41] Holman L. Millennial students' mental models of search: Implications for academic librarians and database developers. The Journal of Academic Librarianship. 2011;**37**(1, 1):19-27

[42] Qayyum DM, Smith DD. Changing research behaviours of university students with progression throughout a course. Journal of the Australian Library and Information Association. 2018;**67**(3):256-277